PRISM OF PERSPECTIVES

THE LIFE AND NAMES OF KWAME GYAMFI

KWAME GYAMFI   JAN BRETZ   OLUSEYE FAKINLEDE

S.C. HUDDLESTON   LASHAWNDA NIMOX

CINDY CONGER

ILLUSTRATED BY
SOFYA WHITE

Prism of Perspectives:
The Life and Names of Kwame Gyamfi

Kwame Gyamfi with
Jan Bretz, Oluseye Fakinlede, S.C. Huddleston, LaShawnda Nimox, and Cindy
Conger

Published by Asya Publishing House
Lincoln, Ne

ISBN Print: 979-8-218-63257-1

Library of Congress Control Number: Pending

Subjects:

BIO002010 BIOGRAPHY & AUTOBIOGRAPHY / African American & Black
BIO026000 BIOGRAPHY & AUTOBIOGRAPHY / Memoirs
BIO000000 BIOGRAPHY & AUTOBIOGRAPHY / General

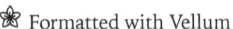 Formatted with Vellum

FOREWORD

Time is the ultimate force in my life. Without time, I would not have family, love, money, experiences, or anything else I consider valuable. Like most people, I did not understand the value of time until it was taken away from me. Nowadays, when I speak to students, one of the first things I say is how much I value time, and I promise I won't waste theirs if they stay focused and listen. With that in mind, I say thank you for taking the time to read this book. My hope is that by the time you are done reading it, you will be inspired to continue your journey. If time is to be appreciated, it is during our lifetimes that we should seek to make it last as long as possible by never giving up.

I did not want to write this book. Initially, it took me several years and gentle nudges from those close to me who knew my background to start the process. Only because of time did that process lead to this unique way to follow my life's story. I do not look at myself as someone special or different. I always say that there are people who have gone through so much more than me that deserve your attention. Yet my experience in psychology tells me that pain is not an exclusive proposition. No one person owns the rights to pain, and every person endures pain in their own way. I am reminded not to look at the measure of my pain but how I can help someone else deal with theirs.

As the premise and format for this book came together, I was forced to confront many demons from the past. I sat with a talented group of writers for fourteen hours of interviews. I want to say thank you to all the writers involved: Jan Bretz, Oluseye Fakinlede, S.C. Huddleston, and LaShawnda Nimox. I want to give a special thanks to the editor Cindy Conger for her encouragement, skills, and guidance in completing this book.

During the interviews, I remembered things long forgotten. I was constantly reminded of the ripple effect we have on other people's lives. Those ripples have positive and or negative ramifications. I think about the people that my poor decisions have had a negative effect on all the time. To them, I say I am sorry; you did not deserve that. I swore to myself many years ago that my legacy would not be about my mistakes but my achievements. We don't know what happens after we die; no one has been able to come back and tell us. What we do know for sure is what we have left behind in the memory of others—that ripple effect. You will be remembered in either a positive or negative light depending upon others' experiences with you and the people you have influenced. Many people will not be remembered at all. One of my biggest fears is not being remembered in a positive light. My definition of heaven and hell is how one is remembered.

Some would say I have lived several lives. I have met many amazing people along the way who did not make this book. There was not enough room to speak about everything I have done or everyone I have encountered, primarily because I wanted to focus on the overall journey and the lessons that can be learned. I have done my best to change the names of everyone written about in this book, with a few exceptions. Those exceptions are people I greatly admire and who have had the most enduring impact on my life. I wanted to honor them. They know who they are. I don't talk in-depth about my love for boxing or hip-hop music growing up. Many stories of racism were excluded because those stories can be heard over and over again every day in America. There was much loss along the way; young lives taken before life truly had meaning. I often see their faces in my mind, a constant reminder of why I do what I do.

When you close this book for the final time, all I ask is that you reflect on your life and ask yourself how your time was spent. Then, I want you to go out into the world and have a positive impact on the people you come in contact with. Remember that what you see on the outside does not always reflect what is being carried around on the inside, so give people the positive energy they may need in that moment. Once again, thank you for your time.

-Kwame Gyamfi

INTRODUCTION

WITH CINDY

What is a story but one person's retelling of a moment or a series of moments? When enough of these moments are shared one upon the other, they create a picture of a year, a decade, a life. We put them in books and call them memoirs.

But what if those same moments could be viewed through a prism? What if, instead of just one person telling their truth, we change our point of view? We incline our head slightly or cast our gaze downward or even close our eyes and take a deep breath. Maybe we'll discover new shapes and colors and aromas—new perspectives—that bring depth and richness to the story. Maybe we'll find connections between my story and yours.

In the spring and summer of 2024, I sat with gifted writers and told my story. In a series of interviews, I described being abandoned as a child, experiencing foster care, adoption, gang violence, and prison, and discovering sports, beauty, and love. I told of the power of identity and name.

And then I asked what they saw.

What resonated with the poet who grew up rough in Chicago or the young journalist from Nigeria? How would the woman who has taught storytelling to generations tell my daughter's birth? Could a man born in a small Midwest town find intersection and interest in our common experience with abuse and abandonment?

In the following pages, you will read my story, vignettes from one man's life that come not just from my point of view but from five of us who each bring our background and perspective, our talent, and our ideas to the narrative.

Now, I offer the story to you, richer, deeper, and more colorful than I might have told on my own. So lean in. Find the threads that are evocative or startling or even familiar. Ask yourself, who is Kwame Gyamfi?

TIMELINE

TIMELINE OF KWAME GYAMFI'S LIFE SO FAR

1974 - Born in Alexandria, Virginia

1976 - Placed in Orphanage in Manassas, Virginia

1978 - Adopted by Mixed-race Parents

1980 - Moved to Omaha, Nebraska

1988 - Moved to 22nd and Sprague Streets in North Omaha

1990 - Ran Away and Lived on the Streets for One Month

1990 - The Hostess Factory Heist

1990 - Boys Town

1992 - Moved to Bellingham, Washington

1994 - Returned to North Omaha

1994 - First Son Born

1996 - Robbery Conviction

1998 - Work Release

1999 - Daughter Born

2002 - Moved to Virginia

2003 - Moved Back to Lincoln

2003 - Married

2008 - Began Coaching Football

2011 - Began Working for Lincoln Public Schools

2021 - Trip to Ghana, West Africa

ABANDOMENT

MY FAMILY TREE begins with me.

That's what I would tell the young boy whose face flashed on the television screen, a poster child for children in the system who were available for adoption. That boy had a different name than the one I use now. *Shannon*. A name that never sat right, that felt like it belonged to someone else. Someone with a different story.

I, that boy who was called Shannon, will always like McDonald's. The sight or smell of one takes me back to my earliest memory. The Department of Social Services in Alexandria, Virginia, sent a cab to pick me up and take me to McDonald's. One of the employees sat with me while I waited for the van from an orphanage to pick me up. It's a fuzzy memory, but it's one of the first when people were sweet to me. The food there is not great for you. I know that, but I still love McDonald's.

Until I was in my thirties, I had no knowledge of my history other than that early memory. I had no idea why I was named Shannon. I didn't know my last name or anything about my parents, although I had applied to receive my adoption history in 2007. Seven or eight years went by—I'd even forgotten all about my request—when, out of the blue—I received a call asking if I was still interested in the information. Absolutely! I was on a quest to discover who I had been so I could know who I truly am now.

The voice on the phone explained that the person who previously held the position with the courts had retired, and my file had been lost in the shuffle.

Lost in the shuffle.

How many hard stories have that in common?

I hung up with a new sense of hope. When the manilla envelope arrived a week later, my heart sank. The documents were incomplete because this had been a closed adoption. Details such as names could only be released if officials had permission from a close living relative. The problem was there were none. I was looking at a blurry photocopy with lines blacked out. "Redacted." I didn't even learn my last name. Yet, from the scant information, I was able to piece together a picture of a mother not equipped to deal with her four children, a mother who had been a victim of abuse and chaos herself. I learned my father was from South Carolina and my mother from Alexandria, Virginia. My birth father was not my mother's first relationship. She'd had two older boys, and my little brother and I also had different fathers.

Included in the report was an account of a police officer on his beat in Alexandria who'd found a boy playing in the streets. The boy tells the officer he lives up the block. The officer escorts the boy to the apartment, where he finds two-and-a-half-year-old me, my six-month-old little brother, and another boy about four. The officer waits for an hour, and my mother never shows up, so he takes us into protective custody. Our mother did appear for the court hearing, retained custody, and then proceeded to have two more reported times where she left us abandoned. The final straw, according to the report, was when she left us with a neighbor and didn't come back for twenty-four hours or something like that. The major complaint was the children were being left alone in their apartment. Other areas of concern were the mother's poor housekeeping, poor management of money, inconsistent mothering, and follow-up of medical care.

The fuzzy black print on the photocopies gave me a pretty clear picture: "On occasion, she could be warm and loving, but just as quickly, she could holler and spank, which was confusing to the children."

My mother ignored suggestions about how to obtain relief. They gave her multiple opportunities to get it together. Kids in this situation today would have been pulled from their homes a lot sooner. They gave my mother opportunity after opportunity. They contacted the grandmother, and she said she didn't know where her daughter was and that her daughter was a bad mother.

When I read this, I asked myself, "How much did the grandmother help? Was she a guiding force or a source of the problem?" She was quick to judge my mama and clearly didn't like her. The paperwork says the mother—my mother—was abused. So, I doubt the grandmother was squeaky clean, even though she had taken in my two older half-brothers. My mom left no forwarding address when we were placed into protective care. But she did call and ask for a visit after she lost custody. She never showed up.

Obviously, she did not really want us.

So, I was transported from the McDonald's of my first memory to an orphanage called The Farm. My little brother went to a more specialized care facility for infants, and for more than two years, until we were adopted together, I lost track of him.

My mother was a teenager when she had the two older boys and twenty-four when she had me. I found out she'd struggled with drug addiction and mental health issues. In one of the incidents when the officers came to our house, the report said they found a big pile of snacks—like she got a bunch of crap snacks and put them in a big pile on the floor, so we had some food we could get to. The officers found me drinking out of the toilet because we didn't have any water we could reach. This became a coping mechanism for me for probably two or three years after that happened. When I was having nightmares or high anxiety or freakouts, I'd end up drinking out of the toilet.

Apparently, my birth father was stabbed to death, and my mother died of a drug overdose. While still leaving many gaps, the documents did give me some sense of relief. I now had a glimpse of my history—some of it a surprise. I thought I was the oldest child, and finding out I had other brothers was a big deal.

I cried when I read the reports but was more angry than sad. I felt pain in my chest, a sinking—almost like I'd dropped into a hole. There was no bottom to the hole, and I was just falling. That feeling stayed with me for some time. I wasn't just angry at my mother and father. I was angry at the environment. I was mad about having to be more than thirty years old before I found out this stuff. There was anger but also a sense of comfort and enlightenment. I understood better where some of my behaviors and issues came from. The first four years of my life, when growth and nurturing are so important—I just didn't have those people. It took some time for me to realize that the things that happened made me who I am. Without that history, I'm not the Kwame who is here today. To this day, I love snacks. I'm a good cook and a foodie now, but I still eat at McDonald's sometimes.

CHAPTER
TWO

WITH JAN

A FEW YEARS AGO, I mailed my saliva to ancestry.com, and several people popped up with close DNA matches. One of these reached out to me, saying, "You know we are probably cousins—maybe even first cousins. Other people who matched told me they couldn't figure out which male in the family was my father, but they thought it was one of two gentlemen. It no doubt raised some ruckus—me popping out of nowhere over forty years later. A lot of the close matches are people living in the same areas in Virginia or South Carolina as my parents. I'm even Facebook friends with some of my newly discovered relatives. I guess that's one of the good things that can come from social media. At some point, I am going to take a trip to meet these cousins of mine, the ones I know for sure are related because of DNA. Meeting them will be like a bookend, a finishing dot.

Besides meeting those people, I want to have a better idea of my mother's history. I want to visit The Alexandria Museum of Black History. I know the city became one of the largest slave trading sites in the country and is listed in the National Register of Historic Places. President George Washington owned a house in a part of the city known since gentrification as Old Town. He stayed there prior to the Revolution. His family home, Mount Vernon, is less than ten miles south. Robert E. Lee's boyhood home in Alexandria sold in 2023 at a reported loss of $70,000 for a price of 4.2 million dollars. Not sure I will see that.

By 1870, Blacks outnumbered Whites in Alexandria. They established Black churches, schools, and other institutions. The still-standing Parker-Gray school, one of the early schools for Black children, was established in 1920. It was closed in 1965 after Brown vs. Board of Education in Kansas declared segregation unconstitutional. It's possible my birth mother attended that school. According to a New America interview with Michael Johnson, Community Leader and Activist in Alexandria, "The books [we read] were like *Jack and Jill, Fun with Dick and Jane*, books like that. But either the front covers were ripped off or the word *monkey* was written in there or [the N-word]. But that's what we had to work with." Johnson, born in 1956, was younger than my mom, so this would have been her experience in elementary school.

Every year Alexandria commemorates the lynchings of two Black teenagers: Joseph McCoy, accused of raping a ten-year-old White girl in 1897, and Benjamin Thompson, accused of criminally assaulting an eight-year-old. These were two of thousands of lynchings throughout the country. In 1939, one of the first sit-down strikes occurred in Alexandria, which was planned by attorney Samuel Tucker, a graduate of Howard University. Five young African American men entered the "public" library and asked for a library card. They were charged with disorderly conduct. I wonder if my mom would have been attending school in 1969 when Alexandria public schools canceled Friday night football games because of vandalism and racial tension. The movie *Remember the Titans*, released in 2000, starring Denzel Washington, told the story of the tinderbox created when three schools segregated and forced the Titans to become a cohesive winning team. Win they did. The Titans from T. C. Williams High School finished their season second in the nation. Photographer Bob Luckett said, "I often think about what kind of ambassadors the Titans could be today. The coaches used to tell us: 'Look, we don't care what you go on to do in your life. We care how you do it. Be professional. Take care of your family. Do the right thing.'" I share his philosophy.

My mother, I think, would have known of the killing of 19-year-old Robin Gibson in a 7-Eleven in 1970 and the protests following in Alexandria. She might have been aware of the resistance to desegregation that forced the closing of public swimming pools as early as the 50s and 60s. Rather than swim with Negros, the city shut down pools, and Blacks swam in the Potomac or the Huntington River. When my mother was a little girl, she would have known that Blacks were expected to walk on one side of the street, and Whites on the other, would have drunk from a designated water fountain and been refused service in most restaurants. Crime rates in Alexandria and many American cities were on the rise between 1960 and 1990s, including incidents of burglary, theft, assault and robbery, and violent crimes. Drug-related crimes rose as well, related to the growing drug epidemic. Studying the history of Alexandria and imagining my mother living it adds to my understanding of what she faced. And perhaps I can now recognize her struggles and humanity as I read between the blurry lines of redacted government documents.

ADOPTION

THAT'S how it went down. I ate from a pile of snacks on the floor and drank from a toilet. The police took us into protective custody, and I went to The Farm. Sometime later, my face ended up on TV, where my soon-to-be adoptive mother saw it. Sometimes, I imagine those early years as historical fiction or a made-for-TV movie. So, I turned the details over to a fiction author and asked him how he'd tell it. What story would he spin about the boy who didn't know his last name?

1976: Manassas Orphanage—The Farm

Manassas, Virginia, is known to others for its part in two bloody battles between the Union North and the Confederate South. Women lost their fathers, sons, and brothers in the name of freedom or industry, depending on the side. The pro-slave state remembers with landmarks and museum exhibits galore. Statues, plantations, and rose gardens, too. My first memory of the place from which I hail—my first core memory at all, really—is climbing up into the back seat of a cab on a cool autumn day. I was only knee-high at the time. I was on my way to another landmark: the Golden Arches of our local McDonald's. The officers said I'd get a hot meal before a nice lady would come and take me away. There's nothing like those greasy McMuffins or some syrupy pancakes to ameliorate a child's mind. I still eat them today. Ba da ba ba baa … you know how it goes.

The cab wasn't yellow like the ones you see on television, swarming like bees through New York City's concrete jungle; mine was blue and white and looked like a big boat with a roof and wheels. The driver, a burly man with a toothpick dangling from his lip and dried skin flaking from the sides of his mouth, held the door for me and buckled me in. I focused with my eyes and fingers on the cracks in the polyester beneath me so that I wouldn't have to look at him, though he seemed nice enough. The boat rocked when he took his seat at the wheel. He adjusted his rear-view mirror to show me his sad eyes and say, "Sorry about this, kid."

I didn't know why he was sorry at the time. I didn't know that the last time an officer found my older brother roaming the streets of my neighborhood on a school day was the last chance for my mother—the only mother I knew back then. She'd left a lot, sometimes for days. So, I didn't eat much other than the pile of snacks she'd sometimes leave on the floor. And the only water I could reach was in the toilet. I guess I knew enough to survive when I got thirsty; the water helped with the rumbling in my stomach. That mother would eventually die of a drug overdose. And I'd later find that the man who fathered me bled to death after being stabbed. I had a younger brother, too. Same eyes and nose and teeth as me, the rest of him just a blur in memory. He went another way, off toward some other landmark, and I wouldn't see him again for quite some time.

I warmed up to the cabbie as he drove, though he did all the talking, that toothpick bobbing up and down with his words. He said I'd be safe soon. That no one would hurt me. I was confused. Had someone hurt me in the past? I was just a kid, a toddler, really. I gazed at the passing yellows, reds, oranges, and purples beneath the gray sky backdrop of fall in the South until we'd reached our destination.

The cabbie walked me into the restaurant and found me a spot in a booth near the front. He said something to a woman behind the counter and sat down across from me. He gazed out the window, toothpick still in place, and waited.

The woman from the counter approached me with a tray of food, asked if I was hungry. I shook my head up and down with vehemence. Pancakes, eggs, one hashbrown disc, plenty of syrup, and a cold orange juice to wash it all down.

I hardly noticed when the cabbie gave me another sad look and a pat on my shoulder. He was off in his boat to retrieve his next fare. I'd never see him again.

The people in that burger joint were some of the nicest I've ever met. They were sure to take turns checking on me every few minutes. And each time, I offered a pancakes-and-egg smile in response. They'd chuckle and move on. One woman went so far as to drape her arm over my shoulders, her hip against the corner of my booth just so. I didn't mind.

The nice lady the officers had told me about showed up while I munched. She ordered some food for herself and sat with me. She told me she worked at the orphanage. She called it "The Farm." She said they had lots of chickens. She said I'd love it, that life would be different from now on. I kept on munching. She gave me some of her juice when I'd finished mine.

WITH FULL BELLIES, the nice lady drove as I rode in another back seat to the land of chickens. I perked my body and craned my neck to see out my window as those squat birds scurried across the long dirt drive up which we rumbled. There must have been hundreds of them clucking about, strutting their stuff. Long trunks topped with vivid leaves of peach and red lined the borders of the property, the biggest yard I'd ever seen. The house on the hill at the top of our path was white with blue shutters, two stories high, and had a wrap-around porch with pearly pillars that jutted to the rafters. Jack-o'-lanterns with triangle eyes and toothy grins covered the railing and steps. On the ground in front of the steps stood a portly woman who shepherded several boisterous children behind her when she saw us coming.

"That's Miss Bailey," the nice lady said. "They're all waiting for you."

I wanted to go back home.

ON MY FIRST night in that house at The Farm, I dreamed ...

A woman: old, almost skeletal, with wrinkles hanging from her bones and a gloating grin. Flashes from the storm through my window show her moving —floating—toward me in a disjointed, silent gait. The only sound the patter of rain turned horizontal from a whispering wind. And breathy laughter, from her or the wind, I cannot tell.

At once, she hovers over me with crooked fingers. Another flash reveals her wholly, unholy, wicked. I squeeze my eyelids and pull on my blanket, but it won't move; it's weighted down by her presence, so I can't cocoon myself in safety. I hope she'll be gone when I open my eyes, but I know she won't. The laughter turns to a chortle, and I know it's coming from her sagging throat.

I feel her fingers upon me, crawling, tickling. Her chortle now a boisterous guffaw. I tremble and pull on my blanket with all my strength. It doesn't budge.

And when I open my eyes, I see black and drooling gums that used to hold teeth, a nose as gnarled as the rest of her, and dark strands of hair that seem to be reaching for me, too. I kick. I scream. But the tickles won't stop. The laughter is all I hear.

I woke in a puddle. Beneath my wet blankets, I prayed—my first mother taught me enough to know God—that I'd never dream again. I kept on praying until sunlight came to save me.

MISS BAILEY WRINKLED her nose and told me to change my clothes before sitting at the long table in the kitchen the following morning. The other kids—seven of them altogether—smiled wryly and snickered and knew why I'd smelled of piss and sweat. Miss Bailey hushed them, but they didn't listen. They shoved vampire teeth in their mouths and wax lips onto their faces and taunted me with ghost sounds: Boo's and ooo's. Halloween was approaching quickly, and everyone else seemed more accepting of the spirits it would bring. There were plastic spiders in faux webs strung about, uncarved pumpkins and gourds on the counters, and stickers on the windows that portrayed witches flying on their brooms, electrified black cats with green eyes, and other ghouls and goblins ready to scare.

Breakfast was eggs, scrambled and plated, with one piece of buttered toast and fried apple slices, served with a glass of milk. I don't recall ever seeing or smelling such morning bounty before that day. I started shoveling mouthfuls. One of the other boys spooned some eggs and flicked them at me when Miss Bailey left the room for some other chore. I'd come to find that Miss Bailey was always choring. Everyone laughed as I picked my fresh shirt clean. All but the girl who sat next to the flicker; she slapped him on the arm, told him he'd die if he tried it again. She was older than the rest of us. The table ooo'd again, but for a different reason, and the flicker's face turned as red as the berries on a Virginia greenbrier in September.

"Come on," said my defender, her voice just as stern with me. She pushed out her chair and walked around to my side of the table. She wore a floral dress over pink, tattered leather t-strap shoes, nappy roots, a black spider ring, and she held out an extra pair of wax lips for me. Her arms were scarred like she'd run through a bramble.

I scarfed a few more bites of my fried apples, took the lips, and followed her obsequiously outside to where the chickens roamed. More ooo's from the table, a different reason yet.

"I'm Bridgett, but people call me Biddy," she said as we walked into the crisp autumn breeze. "What's your name?"

I shrugged my shoulders. I didn't know her yet, and I was a quiet kid anyway.

"Well, I heard Miss Bailey call you Shannon when you got here."

I shrugged again and added a nod.

"Would you like to be friends, Shannon?

I nodded again. And from that moment on, friends we were.

One of the larger, darker chickens waddled up to us, bobbing his head as he came.

"I call this one Brain. He's got attitude, likes to boss the other chickens around, but he's nice to me." She tossed him some pieces of the toast she'd pocketed in her dress from breakfast.

"Why Brain?" I dared to speak and watched as the bird gobbled up his treat.

"Why not?" She handed me some toast, too.

And I supposed that was a good enough reason. I tossed the toast to Brain, and I could tell he wanted more. This was routine.

"More tomorrow," Biddy said, so Brain scampered off to cluck orders elsewhere.

———

A FEW WEEKS in at The Farm, I had a dream that was worse than the first …

A tornado whirls wind out beyond the trees and shakes the house and me maliciously. I think the porch will give, the side of the house, too, and that the tornado will suck me out into the inky black, starless sky and drop me dead in some tall grass where no one can find me. And in the corner of my dark, trembling room, that decrepit woman shows her evil, toothless grin again.

She moves slowly and watches me squirm as her laughter grows louder and louder. And when she reaches me, I see she's worse off than before. The skin on her face is falling off, oozing like wax near a flame. Long bugs with many legs crawl from her eyes and the nostrils of her crooked nose into her mouth and ears and down her neck. She reaches with her tickling fingers that are now nothing more than hard, white bone. I can't escape, although I try. I can't move, and I still see her when I close my eyes. She's in my head. I open my mouth, try to yell for help, but nothing comes out. She's taken my voice, my breath. I grow dizzy and cold, and her laughter echoes.

I woke to screams and realized they were mine. And for a moment, I thought the woman was still there, still tickling me, but it was Biddy who stood next to my bed, trying to rub comfort into my chest. I swatted her hand away.

"It's okay," she whispered. "It's me. There ain't nothing going to get you in this house."

I calmed myself the best I could, chasing my breath, wiping my eyes to be sure it was Biddy.

"You can come sleep with me if you want, but you have to leave before morning. And change first."

In her bed across the hall, and in the glow of a nightlight plugged into the wall, I pointed at her scars, asked with my eyes. I wanted to know how she got them.

"Some people are mean," was all she said. She closed her eyes and started snoring after that, and I figured I'd just let it be.

I prayed next to her warm body for the power to control my dreams if they were to keep coming. I prayed for her scars. Then I prayed for no tornadoes.

———

KWAME: The dreams were real. The Farm and the chickens were real. I remember feeling safe, but I missed my brother and had no idea where he was or if I'd see him again. I was at The Farm for almost two years. I'm sure I made some friends in my own quiet way. Biddy represents those other kids in the system, kids like me, on a journey from and to places we didn't choose.

Back to the movie.

ONE MORNING, after fall and winter had passed at The Farm, some people showed up in a van with big cameras on tripods and even bigger spools of film. They held long poles with microphones on the end covered with fluff to make them look like giant Q-tips. They wore collars and skirts and rolled-up sleeves and hats to shade them from the warmth of spring. Some had headphones over their ears, coiled cords down their backs. One of them unfolded a chair, plopped it in the dirt, and told everyone else where to set things up, clucking orders like Brain.

"Who are they?" one boy asked as all of us kids gathered in excitement. There was sure to be a spectacle.

"Don't get your hopes up," Biddy said. "They ain't going to take us to new homes." Sanguine hearts existed in us all, and hers had been broken too many times.

"No, ma'am," Miss Bailey replied, giddy, wiping her hands on the rag hanging from her waist. "But they're going to put you on the television so good folks who might want to take you in will see you." She let out a deep breath. "All right, now, settle down. Y'all just do what they ask, and if you do it right, we might just find you a family."

Family. I let the word sink in. I hadn't thought of mine in some time.

Family was a tough word for any of us to swallow, really. We'd all had one once, though some of us remembered better than others. Some of us missed the people who brought us into the world; some of us, like Biddy, could do without. I guess we were the spectacle.

The man with the chair approached us and greeted Miss Bailey by removing his hat and nodding slightly. He wore thick glasses and mutton chops. "I think we're ready for you," he said. "We'll want a few group shots, and then we'll have a couple of 'em play around a bit. How's that sound, kids?"

None of us responded.

"That sounds just fine to me," Miss Bailey said.

"Well, all right then." He returned to his chair, made a frame with his hands, and told us all to move a little to his left so we were just in front of the house. Then he asked Miss Bailey for a word, so she walked over to him and didn't come back after.

"Don't look so happy," Miss Bailey called out, but she was the only one smiling.

"Perfect," said the man. "Roll the camera."

Afterward, one of the women who stood behind the man in the chair picked Biddy out of our group, then she asked for another volunteer. Biddy pointed at me.

"He'll do just fine," the woman said. "The rest of you can play in the background."

Everyone stood still.

"Go on, now. Go play," Miss Bailey called. "But leave the chickens alone, hear."

The woman sat Biddy and me right down in the dirt, a little closer to the cameras. She told us to draw pictures with our fingers. A man held one of the giant Q-tips over our heads.

I just knew Miss Bailey would have us clean up before dinner—she liked us clean at the table—but we did as we were told.

"Perfect," said the man in the chair. "That boy's our poster child. Start wide with both," he clucked, "then zoom into him."

We drew simple shapes—the best we could manage with our little fingers in the dirt—hearts and stars, stick people and dogs. It didn't take long at all.

"Got it," said the man in the chair. "Thanks, kids. You're all done. Now we'll get some shots of the area, the chickens and what not. We should be out of your hair within the hour."

"Take your time," Miss Bailey said. "How about some tea?"

"That'll be just fine."

Before the crew left—the man in the chair called them a crew—they gave us suckers. We licked them up as we watched them drive away.

"Y'all just wait," Miss Bailey began, "we'll see you on the television in no time."

———

SOMETIME NEAR THE end of my stay at The Farm, I dreamed again ...

Tickles startle me from a deep sleep. In my threadbare consciousness and through blurry eyes, I see that I've missed her approach, the floating gait of that decrepit woman who haunts me in the moonlight and hides from the sun. I hardly notice the shaking of the house, foundation, walls, and roof shivering in the pelting rain and the tornadoes beyond my window that put grooves in the ground like this malevolent woman's bone fingers in my guts. I shrivel and kick and scream, but she pins me with one hand and places the other on my throat in a slimy grip. She means to end me this time, and Biddy isn't around to save me.

Then her laughter begins, filling my mind and the world around me as I struggle to breathe, to take in air and scream it away, to live. Pressure builds in my temples as my vision fails. It takes all I have to focus, to calm myself, to think my way to survival. I must act. So, I chop my unpinned arms repeatedly. Chop. Chop. Chop. And each time, I feel her rotted skin. I see her resolve melting away like the rest of her until, at last, her chokehold loosens, and I take in a breath that comes back out in a cough.

Ten fingers crawl down my body as her laughter continues. She won't stop. She'll never stop.

I steel myself to sit up. I ball a fist and swing it, and it connects. I hear the crack of my white knuckles on her crooked nose, and in a single fell swoop, I silence the laughter emanating from her oozing, undulating neck. And she dissipates like my reflection in a pond when pierced by a pebble.

She's gone.

Next, I turn to the storm, to those twisters in the sky that I know she brought with her.

I unhinge my window without touching it and fly out like Superman into the sky. I wrap each of those tornadoes beneath my arms and spin, and spin, twirling them into one in midair, and I fling the spinning mass up through the clouds and into the stars.

The world is serene, quiet, mine.

I woke smiling and dry. I'd never dream of that wrinkly woman again.

———

OUR COMMERCIAL WAS BROADCAST weeks after the camera crew shot it, just as Miss Bailey and the man who clucked from his chair said it would. Biddy and I sat together as all of us kids crowded in the living room around the television: a gray glass screen inside a wooden box, a switch and a few knobs on the right of the screen, and an ornate mesh design on the left behind which a speaker pushed sounds of us and our chickens over a melancholic melody. We watched as a woman from the crew spoke of how each of us deserved a family. We saw ourselves playing, Biddy and I drawing pictures in the dirt until the commercial ended with me front and center. A phone number appeared just above my head, the call to action was appealing; tugged just hard enough on the heartstrings of a couple of folks from a few towns over, in Woodbridge.

"You done good," Miss Bailey said. "All of you done good."

———

KWAME: It wasn't quite that Hollywood. There was no film crew or highly produced commercial with a tear-jerking soundtrack like Sarah McLachlan singing about sad animals with big sad eyes. But I was a poster child, and my picture was on TV. My adoptive mom saw it and picked up the phone.

Now the movie turns to her backstory.

TOP: My adoptived dad at his military job. My adoptive mom on an outing to the park.

CENTER: I was reunited with my younger brother when we were adopted.

BOTTOM: I've always loved stylish clothes.

A SECONDHAND STORY: There was a stocky Black man on base to whom others paid heed. Three chevrons and three rockers on his sleeve made him a Master Sergeant, and he was an airborne qualified Green Beret to boot, a certified badass with a temper who ruled with a tungsten fist. After a few days' training in the field, he entered the chow hall famished, ready to eat.

There was a woman who worked in that very chow hall on that very base—German and White with a body she carried with grace and covered with a sort of European elegance. Where on the inside she was stoic, impervious even, on the outside she was, simply, gorgeous. She spent her whole life in Black neighborhoods, unabashed and unafraid. Nothing scared her, especially those foul-mouthed soldiers who crowded her counter with empty bellies and trays, looking to her to fill them. They looked to her for other reasons, too, beautiful as she was.

When that hungry Master Sergeant reached that woman in the chow line, she filled his tray just like the rest with a plop of slop. He was nothing special.

"Next," she said.

"I want another helping," he replied.

"You can have another, if you pay for another."

"Can't you just put some more on?"

"Next." Her countenance unaltered. She didn't have the time or the energy.

"Come on!" he demanded.

She wouldn't. She'd seen enough of him and guys just like him to give in.

"Fuck this," said the man. He smashed his tray on the counter and stormed out of the chow hall.

"Next." She was unfazed.

Plop.

Slop.

Plop.

Slop.

———

LATER THAT DAY, the man returned, head down, sorry eyes staring at the bunch of flowers in his hand that he'd just picked.

"Can I help you?" the woman asked. No smile, but she knew the flowers were for her. Flowers are often freely given to beautiful women, and she'd received many offerings before.

"Well, I … I just wanted to say—"

"Whatever it is, you can look me in the eye to say it."

Snickers came from down the chow line.

"Get fucking moving, privates," the man commanded. He waited for the laughing lower ranks to shuffle by.

Then back to the woman, who had let a smirk slip. "I just wanted to say I'm sorry for the way I acted earlier. It's not often someone tells me no." He handed the flowers over the counter. She took them, but not without trepidation; not for him—she'd seen a thousand of him—but for what she might allow herself to do.

"Well, I suppose you'd better get used to it," she said.

"I don't mind that. I don't mind that at all."

"Good. Something else I can do for you?"

"I hope so," he replied. He stood up straight, took a deep breath. "How would you like to join me for a night off base? I know a great place where we can move a little."

"You going to keep that temper of yours under control?" she asked without hesitation.

"Yes, ma'am."

"I don't dance."

"Me either," he chuckled. "We can just sit and eat."

"I'll be off in an hour."

"I'll be here."

He about-faced with a grin that turned to a wide, white-tooth smile when he heard her say, "Thanks for the flowers."

And that was all it took. Two souls became one on that day. They'd marry soon after at a church right there in Woodbridge, Virginia. They'd buy a green Volkswagen Beetle, drive it out for movies or burgers, and park it in their driveway to enjoy evenings in front of the television; popcorn fights on the couch; farts and giggles; arguments about money, their future, their past; nights of love; nights of hate; sickness and health; and everything else that marriage had to offer.

Then, one day, that man and that woman saw the commercial shot on The Farm. They saw the house, all of us kids, Biddy, and me, and they couldn't resist dialing the number that floated above my head.

"I want him," the woman said, a tear on her cheek, staring into my eyes that flickered on the screen.

"He's a little light," the man replied, referring to the pigment of my skin.

"He's darker than me. You got a problem with me?"

"No, ma'am."

"All right, then." She had a way of settling things.

———

AFTER MY LAST breakfast at The Farm—Miss Bailey gave me an extra helping of her fried apples—I sat with Biddy on the porch. I'd never seen her cry until that day. None of us had. And none of the others dared snicker at her when she did. They stayed far away; let us have our last moments together.

"Brain's gone," she said in a feeble cry.

"Where?" I glanced around at the other birds in the large yard and down the hill.

"He's gone. Dead. Probably in the belly of some coyote or fox."

"Are you sure?" I stood, ready to canvas the area. "We could—"

"I looked before breakfast. He's gone."

"I'm sorry, Biddy."

"Don't matter. Now you're leaving, too."

"I don't want to."

"You got to. Got to get away from here. Start new with a family."

"I'll come back then," I said. "I'll come back and get you."

"You'll forget me."

"I won't. I promise, I won't."

"Everyone does eventually." She was rubbing the scars on her arms. She was far off in some memory. "Everyone leaves."

"How'd you get them, Biddy?"

"My brother ... I couldn't save him."

I waited patiently for her to continue.

"My daddy was mean, and so were his dogs." She sniffled snot as her cries deepened. "'Sic 'em,'" he said. 'Sic 'em.'" And they chased my brother through the pasture. I can still hear him screamin."

I sat next to her again, put an arm around her. She turned and sank her wet face into my chest.

"Daddy called them off after a minute, but it was too late. My brother couldn't see the fence. The grass was too tall, and he was too short." Her chest heaved. "I followed the screams and found him wrapped up in the barbed wire."

"Biddy—"

"I got him out," she cried. "We were both covered in blood. He got sick from it, but I didn't. He died. Nothing happened to Daddy or those dogs, so I ran away."

I wrapped my other arm around her, hugged her tight, and she let me for a moment. Then she pushed me back.

"Go! Don't turn out like my daddy. Like everyone's daddy in this place."

"I won't," I said. "I'll come back."

I wanted her to believe it as much as I wanted it to be true.

But she stood up, wiped her face, and went inside, leaving me alone on the porch.

Miss Bailey came out after.

"She'll be all right," she said. "I'll look after her."

I was crying, too, and Miss Bailey held me until we saw a trail of dust coming in the distance.

Those folks from Woodbridge drove up our long dirt driveway in their green Beetle to take me away, and Miss Bailey told me I should be happy. She said I could finally start my new life, just like Biddy had said. But I'd gotten used to The Farm, the chickens, the good cooking, and Miss Bailey herself. I'd gotten used to having a good friend in Biddy who didn't want me to leave. I didn't want to go.

———

I STUDIED my reflection in the window next to me and thought of those I'd left behind as the Beetle rumbled away, two strangers in the front seats. And before long, like a dream brought on by a brake pedal screech, I saw my face beyond the glass as well—my eyes and nose and teeth on a Black boy who walked hand in hand with an unfamiliar woman to meet us as we came to a stop. Something inside me stirred—a blur of memory. Two years was a lifetime.

My brother.

I knew it before my adoptive mother let me out of the car to say as much.

She sobbed and smiled. She said, "When I found out … we had to have you both." She nudged me closer to him. She waited.

I looked at him, and he looked at me. We studied, assessed and measured, and spoke without words in a way that only siblings can. Like no one else existed. Then, he chuckled and put his arm around me the way Biddy sometimes did when we'd smuggle food from the kitchen to the chickens.

"Well, what do you think?" asked our adoptive father, gesturing toward our new front door, pride in his eyes and chest. His wife moved to him with more sobs of gratitude and embraced him.

Together, my brother and I turned. We took it all in.

We had a home: red and brown bricks under a shingled roof, an attached garage with a tan door with four little windows that were too high for me to see through, a paved driveway coming from a paved street over which trees towered all the way along the sidewalks. Concrete steps and a black rail led from that green VW Beetle up to the front door. And through the house and through the back door, my second core memory: Frogs. Hundreds of them—millions to my young eyes—ribbiting as they dove into the recessed pool or leaped out of it into what was our new back-yard, which came complete with a large weeping willow in the corner. There were other kids in the neighborhood, too. Right over the fence—in a backyard of their own—two girls with long ponytails. Those girls—whose mother had just walked my brother to me—would later babysit us while our new parents were at work or on one of their non-dancing dinner dates.

Parents: a word I could use now. Again? Finally.

ABUSE

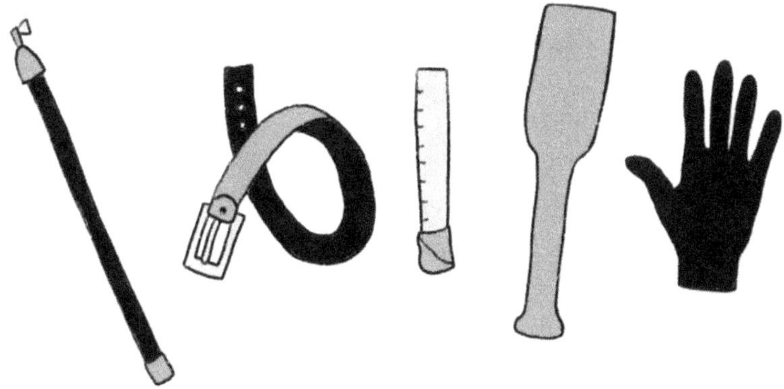

CHAPTER
SIX
WITH S.C

CHILD ABUSE and neglect is not a competitive sport. By that, I mean it doesn't matter if the abuse and neglect are harsher or more severe and even more observable than what goes on across town or across the street. Abuse and neglect, in any measure, leave a child with wounds and later scars. I can say that from the perspective of a fifty-year-old man looking back at the twelve years I lived in my adoptive parents' home. My name was now Shannon White. It was the first time I remember having a last name, but it didn't fit me. Shannon always sounded like a girl's name, and I certainly wasn't White. Home didn't fit me either. It was not a place of unconditional love—a place where I could explore the world and learn who I was. It was not a place of stability or safety. And when my daddy found religion, it got worse.

The movie rolls on.

OUR ADOPTIVE FATHER was nice at first. He'd wrap our little bodies up in his muscular arms, tickle us, make us laugh in high-pitched squeals. He'd take the thick black frames off his face and put them on ours and turn our vision blurry. But he was transactional, his Master Sergeant to our grunt; all those tickles and laughs came at the price of sweat equity in the form of endless chores. Family was work, his approval the paycheck.

I'd soon learn that he was happiest when he was fishing or drinking, and especially when doing both. And he was happier yet when gambling in the company of his military buddies. But he had a sailboat, and he'd take us out on the Potomac to drown some worms for blue cats or drag a lure for bass. He taught us to fish, and I loved him for it.

FROM BENEATH OUR white sail that pointed to a sunny blue sky, I gazed at the rocky shores and the lush treetops beyond them as we slipped through the river's rushing water in our slender boat. The breeze was calm but enough to push us, and the birds were plenty, singing morning songs, wishing us luck, and hoping for their own feasts. I wondered then about Biddy and Miss Bailey and all the other kids. Birdsongs on The Farm weren't so different. I think everyone and everything is hoping for something—food or family, sunlight to save us from the night.

My new father sat next to me and brought my attention back to the moment.

"You off in La La Land again?" He'd just rigged up a couple of rods for my brother and me and was explaining how to use them while I'd gawked off into the time before him.

I just smiled.

"All right, we don't use closed reels with buttons in this family," he said as he demonstrated how to use what he called a proper reel. "One more time: you hold the line with your pointer finger, like this, then you flip the bail, aim at where you want your bait to drop, then when you cast, you release the line from your finger at the same time and let it fly." He exaggerated the word "fly," and smiled wide. "One smooth motion. You boys got it?"

"Yes, sir," we said in unison. He told us to call him sir but got angry when his military buddies did it. He'd tell them he worked for a living, and they'd all laugh. I didn't get it.

"All right, then. Now you try."

I was up first, and I could see the relief in my brother's eyes. I took the long rod and proper reel and did my best to emulate what he'd taught us, and when it didn't work, he laughed, a deep laugh from his belly. He took a sip from his drink.

"You've got to release the bail first, son."

"Yes, sir." I liked it when he called me son.

I tried again, and this time, it worked but my worm landed next to me on the boat. He laughed again and shook his head, too.

"You forgot to aim."

"Sorry, sir."

"Don't be sorry. Just relax and do it how I showed you. And remember, let it fly."

I tried again and sank my worm a few feet in front of me.

"There you go." He clapped me on the back. "Now, let the water take it a bit before you flip your bail back over to lock it in."

I did as I was told.

"All right. You'll get better over time. Now keep an eye on your line. Don't get it tangled or snagged. Keep your pole pointed that way, and your brother will cast from the other side."

"Yes, sir."

"Good boy."

My brother cast his worm on the first try, and then nothing happened for ages, it seemed. The three of us just sat together on that slender boat and glided along and walked our worms like dogs on leashes. Dad sipped on beer. He was particularly fond of brandy, but when we were fishing, it was always Heineken. I peered over the edge of the boat and hoped like those singing birds to spot some fish, but I saw nothing. I felt nothing on my line, and neither did my brother or our new father. I started to think that fishing was more about being on the boat, about being together between the bites, about men calling boys sons. And then, the tip of my pole started to bob. My heart dropped to my stomach.

"Atta boy," said our father, with one of his wide smiles. "Now set the hook." He showed me how by flicking his wrist back with his rod in his hands.

"It's strong," I said as whatever was on my line pulled and pulled. The sound of my proper reel's drag clicked like the throats of our frogs back home.

"Must be a big one. Lean back, then reel forward." Again, he showed me with his rig. "Lean back, then reel."

"I can't." I struggled.

"We don't use those words." His voice suddenly stern.

He put his rod in a holder on his side of the boat and reached over to help me pull my rod back between each reel.

"It is a big one." He was giddy. He grabbed a net and set it in the water. "Now lay it right in here so we don't lose it."

I tried my best, but my arms weren't big like his—I thought they'd snap if my pole didn't first—and that fish was a fighter, and it thrashed hard at the water's surface when I finally got it near the net. We saw a white belly flip into the net and then out again. My brother gasped. My line went loose; coils slipped through the rings on my rod. My father sighed. I lost it.

"Damnit," he shouted. "He spit it out."

"I'm sorry," I said, ready to cry. Surely, I'd done something wrong. "I tried."

We were all silent for an awful lot of minutes. Then I whispered, "Can I try again?"

He grabbed my pole, tied a fisherman's knot, and set up my rig again.

WHEN WE PULLED up back at the house, my adoptive mother was waiting outside the open garage with inculpatory eyebrows raised high and holding a lifejacket in each hand.

"Shit," Dad said.

"What is it?" my brother asked.

After a bunch of yelling on Mom's part, apologies on Dad's, and some snickering on ours, we learned that it was a matter of law and safety that we wear those jackets every time we went out on the boat. She made sure we never forgot them again.

OUR NEW MOTHER, that staunchly stubborn and gorgeous woman, showed us what it felt like to love and be loved. She was stern, just like her husband, but she'd developed a soft spot for me the moment she looked into my flickering eyes in that Adopt a Kid commercial. She'd take my brother and me out for walks most days after work.

"Take a picture, it'll last longer!" she'd say to the rubbernecks who disagreed with her interracial family. It always made me laugh, though she'd always tell us to quit laughing and keep walking. Sometimes my brother and I would break into spontaneous dancing, jigging, and jiving with my mom standing by smiling.

She'd tuck us in at night in our very own room—something I was grateful for after my time at The Farm. We had twin beds with Star Wars sheets and glow-in-the-dark, puffy stickers on the headboards—Hanna-Barbera, Casper the Ghost, and The Great Grape Ape. She put glow-in-the-dark stars on our ceiling, too, and told us to reach for them always. She laughed when I literally reached for the ceiling. She explained that we could be anything we wanted to be, that there were no limits.

"I WANT to be a soldier like Daddy," I said, my head on my mother's chest as she lay with me in my bed. We stared into those stars—those glowing possibilities—and contemplated my future. My brother lay with us, nuzzled to Mom's hip on the other side of her.

"Oh, you don't want to do that. All them potty mouths. Do something with your brain, baby."

"But Daddy likes what he does," said my brother in my defense.

"It sure seems that way, don't it?" She twirled the hair on the side of my head.

"He doesn't?" I asked.

"I think he did at first. He's seen a lot, and not all of it was good."

"He sure likes being around all those potty mouths."

She chuckled. "Those men are just built different. They come from a different time."

"I think it'd make him proud. Me doing what he does."

"I think you can make him proud without running through the woods with your hair on fire."

I lifted my head to look her in the eyes. "Is that what Daddy does?"

"No," she chuckled again, pulled me back down.

"Maybe I could play football. Or be a coach."

"Coach Shannon. Now there's something I'd like to see."

"I'll make you proud, Momma."

"I'm already proud, baby." She squeezed us. "I'm proud of both of you."

IT TOOK a while for the beatings to start. Dad had a temper when he drank, and he drank a lot. He'd tell us to pick our own switches off the weeping willow tree out back when we forgot to clean up our room or help our mother with some chore or another, and sometimes for no reason at all. We learned quickly that the thinner sticks hurt much worse, and we always took our time picking them out to steel ourselves for the pain. He worked on us quite a bit, too. We were brothers of hurt and loss and reunion, and we took it all together. After a while, I figured out that if I was quick to take the blame or volunteer to go first for the whooping, sometimes my dad would spend his anger on me. I made it a goal to spare my brother as much of the pain as possible.

Mom let Dad raise his family how he saw fit. He never laid a hand on her, though. I guess that was something to be happy about.

TOP: With my brother in our early music days
CENTER: Me about the time we moved to Omaha.
BOTTOM: Pinewood Elementary in Omaha.

DOUGLAS COUNTY, Nebraska, is the birthplace of Malcolm X, Marlon Brando, John Beasley, and several other notable figures. Right there, in the biggest city in the state, Omaha. Today, it's known for its Fortune 500 companies, its cattle trade (finest steaks in the country), the College World Series, and one of the best zoos on the planet, the Henry Doorly. But I've got different memories of the city. Some that make me laugh, and some that still hurt to this day.

This wasn't Virginia. It was more concrete than green. I occasionally heard birds but no frogs. Dad started gambling more and more after we moved to our gray house in the Midwest. He started drinking more, too. I don't think he liked the move, being the Southern man that he was, but orders were orders. And that meant more beatings for my brother and me.

One day, Mom came home from work, frazzled. Her days were long as she tried to do her part for the family. She dropped her purse and jaw as soon as she walked through the front door. We were sitting on the floor in the living room, rolling a ball back and forth across the room, waiting for Mom like normal. Dad was on leave for the day. He was asleep in his room.

"Hi, Momma," I said as I rolled the ball again. I smiled at first but furrowed my brow when she didn't respond. "Momma?"

She looked at my brother and then back to me. She lifted me into her arms and asked, "What happened?"

"What do you mean, Momma?" I thought I'd dried my eyes up pretty well when I heard her car door shut in the driveway.

"What do you mean, what do I mean? How'd you get all these marks—"

Realization slapped her in the face like Dad slapped us boys from time to time.

"Has Daddy been drinking again?"

I hesitated. She was never any good at hiding her emotions. "Yes, ma'am."

"Did he do this to you?"

I looked away. I couldn't stand the regret in her eyes.

Then, to my brother, "Did he do this to him?"

Back to me, "You answer me, boy. And I mean now."

"Yes, ma'am. But–"

She didn't let me finish. She didn't let me say I'd forgotten to pick up my dirty clothes in the bathroom. She put me down and stomped across the room hard and fast into the hall. The front door of our house swung open and closed with the breeze. I hung her purse up and closed the door tight when I took my brother out to the front yard for a bigger game of catch—we didn't like listening to the screams. I saw my reflection in the glass as I pressed the door to latch: welts up and down my arms and legs and face, too. He'd been pinching me that day, between his fingers and the palm of his hand, my drunken Dad. He said with eighty-proof breath that it was all my fault, though he never said what it was. That's when I figured he was mad about the bathroom. When I cried, he pinched more and slapped me a little, told me not to be such a pussy. When my brother yelped in my defense, he got slapped or booted and told to shut it.

Dad said he should have taken me back to the place he'd found me. And believe me, there were plenty of days I wished he would have. I pictured Biddy and Miss Bailey and all the others around that bountiful table in the mornings. All that food. Maybe I could have found Brain if I'd had the chance to look. But then I realized I'd be without Momma and my brother. And I sure would miss them a lot.

When the screaming stopped, Momma rubbed lotion over my wounds and then took us out for burgers and ice cream. There were some golden arches just blocks away, walking distance—I guess that landmark was everywhere by then. And when the man behind the counter stared just before handing us the chocolate and vanilla twist cones, Momma said, "Take a picture, it'll last longer!" I laughed all the way home, and that time, she didn't snap at me for doing it.

We sat on the porch after, lapped at our treats in the waning light of the sun. And so, our tradition continued at the gray house in Omaha, the three of us walking away from the pain and the man who caused it. Sometimes we'd get all the way to the mall six miles down the road. Sometimes we took the bus, but mostly, we walked.

I WALKED to school in those days. One particular morning, I ditched my brother and headed through the neighborhood alone. The sun was warm, but the early morning breeze cool as I jumped over every crack in the sidewalk for the sake of my mother's back, as the old saying dictated. I passed the house that had a great trampoline in the front yard. I hoped the kids there would invite me to try it out sometime, and I hoped they'd place their sprinkler beneath like I'd seen once when we were driving by. As I walked down the street, I heard a woman yelling, out of breath. Then, without seeing the woman herself, I saw the reason for her screams: pointed ears that laid back, a shining chain-link collar cinched above muscles that bulged like my dad's, and sharp, drooling fangs. It was the biggest Doberman I'd ever seen. It was growling, low rumbles I swear I could feel, and it looked hungry for nothing but me.

I ran.

I turned and ran as fast as my little legs would take me, never mind the damn cracks in the sidewalk, or Momma's back, for that matter. She'd understand. If only I could reach her. If I could just make it back to the house and through the door with a quick slam. Momma would send that mean dog back home with its tail between its legs.

But I didn't make it.

Now that I look back on it, I had no chance of outrunning that beast. It was fully grown, and it didn't help that the shouting woman—his master—was chasing him as he chased me. It caught me just as I'd turned to track its pace. It took me down like one of the football players I'd hoped to be one day. My wind was lost, but I had no chance to search for it as those fangs sunk into my ankle. The pain, sharp and shooting up my leg, was more than the slap of any switch or the crack of my father's tungsten fist.

I screamed, but no sound came. It was like the wrinkly woman from my nightmares at The Farm had returned to steal my breath once more.

And then the beast's master pulled him off me as it barked and lunged and nearly pulled her arm out of its socket. She said she was sorry, that he'd had his shots. I didn't know what she'd meant at the time. I just saw the blood. My eyelids were heavy. And then, I saw nothing.

The woman shook me awake after she'd stowed the Doberman. She carried me home, and luckily, she knew my mother, who no one wished to cross.

Momma took me to the emergency room, where my wound was washed and stitched. I still have the crooked, zig-zag scar. I've been wary of dogs ever since.

MY THIRD-GRADE TEACHER, Mrs. Albert, was tall and skinny and always wore dresses with floral button-up tops. Her attire was as colorful as her classroom décor. She had a soft voice, calming. She spoke as if she didn't want to startle me, and she always had lotion for my bruised and blood-blistered hands. Dad used a taped-up ruler to regularly bust our knuckles at home. The welts on my back and shoulders came along as we grew in years. The sting on my flesh numbed after a while. The real pain was in the shower as I washed off the blood that had trickled down my back. It didn't matter how cold I got the water.

After rubbing the lotion in with hands as soft as her spoken words and blowing a soothing breath, Mrs. Albert let me draw pictures to take my mind off things at home. Garfield was my specialty, that orange tabby Persian with his squinted, wry eyes and smirk. I'd create comic strips to mimic those I'd seen on Dad's newspaper from across the breakfast table, but my Garfield was a friend, a hero to my brother and me. The only trouble my cat caused was for the man who hurt us.

"You're getting pretty good at that," Mrs. Albert said when she realized I didn't hear the bell or see my classmates leave for the day.

I was working on a scene where Garfield overcame a particular Doberman, whose house I would avoid on every outdoor excursion for the rest of the time we lived in that little gray house.

I shrugged my shoulders meekly.

"How would you feel about drawing some pictures for me?"

I lit up. "Of Garfield?"

"Actually, I was thinking that you could draw the cover for our Book of the Month."

"I could do that," I said under no uncertain terms. That month's book was, *The BFG*, and I'd already had some doodles of that wonderful giant and little Sophie, who reminded me a lot of Biddy.

"I figured as much." She smiled and put her soft hand on my shoulder.

And so, I drew pictures of Charlotte and Wilbur, Little Bear, the tiny warrior from Omri's cupboard, Frog and Toad, and the apple tree that gave and gave to the little boy—for which I'd received a lot of praise from my classmates and other teachers as well. Mrs. Albert taught me as good teachers do. I'm forever grateful.

Later in elementary school, another teacher would teach me cursive. I was intrigued at first, thinking it was a lot like drawing. But when I rushed through my work, my letters got sloppy, and penmanship became punishment. I had to write a single sentence 100 times, sometimes 200, or five pages, front and back. I can still draw and write in a pretty cursive hand, but I'm much fonder of remembering the teacher who encouraged me to draw.

AGITATION

CHAPTER
EIGHT
WITH LASHAWNDA

IT WAS time to move again, which wasn't a big deal because I'd been on the move most of my young life. This move would prove to be very different. I didn't know what to expect, so I treated it like I'd treated all the other moves. But moving to 22nd and Sprague in North Omaha was the move that, if I were playing chess, would be the point in the game to call checkmate. Checkmate means the king can't escape, and between my abusive home, gang-affiliated neighborhood, and tone-deaf school culture, I was definitely trapped.

From the first day of moving into the neighborhood, I learned I would be challenged. What I considered an innocent ride on my ten-speed bike introduced me to the culture of the area. I immediately learned being asked, "What's up cuz?" wasn't an innocent question or greeting. In fact, it was the opposite. It was a threat. I'd have to fight just to keep my bike from being stolen, and from that day on, I knew I would have to fight to survive. This wasn't like the neighborhood on 63rd Street, but fear wasn't an option for me and was not an emotion I cared to visit. In this neighborhood, showing any sign of fear or weakness puts you at the bottom of the food chain. It was eat or be eaten.

Not too far from our new house, down at the corner of Florence Boulevard and Pratt Street, was Horace Mann Middle School. Across the street, there was a park with basketball courts. The park had a different name. It's Kountze Park now and was even known as Malcolm X Park for a time, but we always called it Horace Mann Park, and it's where stuff went down.

Fighting came easy, not really by choice but more out of being a protector. The protector in me came out one day when my brother was walking our dog Fluffy at the park. He came back to the house and told me some kids were messing with him. Honestly, he didn't need to say anything else. I wasn't going to let anybody mess with my brother and get away with it. We got to the park, and I noticed a small group gathered there, shooting a gun at the trees. I immediately recognized that these were no kids. They were grown-ass adults who were part of a gang.

I walked over, not intimidated by them or their guns or their antics. I told them to leave my little brother alone. Words were exchanged, and I knew we were outnumbered, but I was willing to take the L if it came down to it. I wasn't afraid and I would fight to protect myself and my little brother.

When it comes to my fighting abilities, I acknowledge that my father laid the foundation. He'd often put my brother and me in boxing gloves when we were younger. He taught us to hash out our grievances by boxing each other in the backyard. He also took us to a boxing gym and spent time teaching us the rules. Boxing seemed like my dad's way of trying to connect with us. To me, boxing was a sport. I'd never thought much about putting my boxing skills to use against somebody. I had never had to until we moved into North Omaha; it was the only weapon I had to defend myself.

Surprisingly, nothing happened that day at the park. I didn't even have to raise my fists. That was only the first of many unpleasant experiences I would have at that park. Horace Mann was an epicenter of my time in the hood, but after that day and that particular encounter with the gang, they seemed to treat me differently. It was like they all of a sudden had a level of respect for me, and they also left my little brother alone.

They weren't the only gang in our area. We had all-Black gangs, Hessian gangs, and gangs moving in from the coasts to establish territory. Our forty-block move from 63rd Street introduced us to gangs, which were on the rise in Omaha. My family witnessed a shootout, which fascinated my brother and me but scared my parents. That park across the street from Horace Mann was a breeding ground for violence.

We were playing basketball at the park one day. I was playing half-court when I noticed a dude on the sideline chanting and cheering for the kid I was playing. Every once in a while, he'd throw in little insults at me. It became obvious that I was playing his little brother. He continued to throw jabs at me, and it was only a matter of time before I got fed up. I walked up to him and told him to shut the fuck up, then returned to the court and kept ballin'. Then he said one more thing, and I lost it. I punched him. We were fighting on the court, and his brother joined in, so I was fighting both of them. Hey, I thought, I had a brother here, too. Where the fuck was he?

At some point during this fight, I saw an older dude with a Jheri curl pull up in his Chevy Nova. He gets out of the car, and I thought he was going to join in to make it three-on-one. But he grabbed me by the back of my collar and told me to get off his brother. I think he understood what was going on, so he just pulled us apart.

I found my brother ballin' on another court, and we fled the park. He claimed he hadn't seen any fight. Honestly, I think he was scared, and I don't blame him. That fight in the park added to my reputation. You had to steal on me first because if you didn't, I could guarantee that I was gonna steal off you.

Days at Horace Mann Park were very unpredictable. Gang members had a significant presence, so you had no choice but to deal with them, especially if you were going to be at the park. While I was never more than a wannabe, parts of gang life inspired me. One of the first gang members I met at the park was from Kansas City, and he was the cleanest gangster I had ever seen. He always matched from head to toe. The way he dressed— the fresh cut, all dripped in red with some fresh, all-red FILAs—I remember looking at him and thinking he was what I was trying to become. His fashion was crazy, and he had a walk to match.

I was hanging at the park playing basketball one afternoon when a tan '77 Chevy Impala four-door rolled by real slow. It looked like a hoot ride, a car stolen by a gang member and then used during robberies, shootings, drug deals, or other dirty work. When the car rolled by, I noticed four dudes in the car, and I knew it was a rival gang. The car came around a second time, and one of the dudes was sitting out the window on the passenger side, holding a gun on the roof of the car. He wore a blue baseball cap, and you could see a strap in his hand. Two members of the gang that normally ruled the park started walking toward the car, repeatedly yelling, "What up, Blood?" I, of all people, knew that when that line was spoken, something bad was about to happen. Then the guy sitting on top of the car with the strap yells back, "Blood Killer, cuz!" and starts shooting.

It was complete chaos; everyone scattered in the park, and my brother and I hid behind some trees. There were tons of people in the park, and to this day, I can't believe nobody was shot or killed. But it didn't always go down that way. The first gang-related murder I remember was a stabbing at a local burger joint, and from that point on, it seemed like there was a snowball effect with gangs in Omaha.

While I was trying to adjust to our new neighborhood and gang culture, I also had to prepare to adapt to middle school. From 1970 to 1996, Omaha Public Schools had mandatory bussing. Riding the bus was a first for me. I walked to elementary school from the gray house on 63rd Street. School bus culture was a different beast in itself. I quickly learned the three rules for school bus survival: Fighting, cracking on people (joke), or being invisible. I wasn't good at cracking, and I definitely wasn't going to be invisible. Cracking was a new concept for me and for somebody who didn't have any money, shared clothes with his brother, wore busted shoes, and a bad haircut, I wasn't exactly in a position to talk about nobody, so fighting was my go-to. I only had to prove myself a few times for people on the bus to understand that whooping ass wasn't a problem for me.

The problem was that I could handle myself on the bus and at the park. Defending myself against my father was another matter. The pressure from school and trying to adjust to the neighborhood was already a struggle, so you would think home would be my safe haven. Unfortunately, home was a different kind of nightmare, and I was fighting a different battle at home than in the streets. The beatings from my dad were more intense and more frequent. My mother didn't do anything to help, which made her a part of the problem. My father had become immersed in religion, which only made the beatings worse. I don't know if he was trying to beat the devil out of me or scare me straight, but home was hell.

22nd & Sprague Streets, Omaha

OUR RELATIONSHIP with our adoptive father was always transactional. He demanded discipline and obedience and meted out punishments or rewards as he saw fit. If the dishes didn't pass inspection after washing, we owed him pushups. If bed corners weren't tight or rooms tidied just so, we got beatings. We got paid for a few jobs, like mowing lawns, and my dad set up bank accounts for us, but he would never let us use our money. I was tired of getting cracked on about my clothes; money could change that, and my dad had it just sitting in a bank account. My brother and I somehow found out that we could withdraw the money on our own, which was all the motivation we needed. We decided to take the bus downtown to the bank. We took our money out of the account and went straight to the mall.

It was my time to shine! I needed a few pairs of Dickies to begin to make my fashion statement. I was sure I was about to be as fresh as the gang members I admired. I bought a few pairs of boxer shorts that were the style at the time. I felt good. I was proud of my newly purchased clothing, but I knew there was no way in hell I could take these new clothes home. I wouldn't be able to answer any questions from my parents about where the new clothes came from. With the beatings I was already getting from my dad, there was no way in hell I was gonna add anything else for him to get pissed about.

When we were done elevating our clothing, it was time to implement Operation Cousin House. We decided to keep our new clothes at our cousins' house. They weren't our real cousins—it was one of those situations where we called each other cousins because we grew up together and our families were so close. The plan was to go to their house before school and change into our new fits. Our parents would have no idea about the clothing, and we wanted to keep it that way.

One day, while we were changing clothes, my cousin gave me a bottle of pills. I wasn't sure what he expected me to do with them or why he had them. Little did I know that those pills would open my hustler mentality. My cousin called the pills uppers and told me people typically order them out the back of catalogs but said I could sell the pills and make some money. That's the only thing I needed to hear. I could make some money. Hustler mentality was activated immediately. I had discovered how a little money could change my life, so I took those pills and began selling them at school. I was making a lot of money and had become quite the entrepreneur.

Everything seemed to be going well, and I hoped to end my ninth-grade year at Norris Middle School on a high note until I broke a window in the school hallway while the principal was standing directly behind me. It wasn't unusual for kids with rap music running through their heads to set up a beat on the large plexiglass panels. If you hit them just right, they'd reverberate, and someone down the hall would respond with a beat of their own. We were the hip-hop generation. Hip-hop and rap had been the soundtrack for my life since we moved to 22nd and Sprague. I saved up to buy cassette singles. I tried to find hip-hop songs with a jazz element that I thought my dad might approve of, but he rejected them all. Now, my beat had shattered my summer plans. I spent my vacation scraping gum and cleaning classrooms to pay for that window.

DURING THIS TIME IN OMAHA, ninth grade was still considered middle school. When I returned to school in the fall as a tenth grader, I was in high school for the first time. We were bussed from North Omaha to Burke High School. If you ask Google to map you a route from my house to Burke, it will tell you it's sixteen miles and will take twenty-four minutes if you take Dodge Street, which is Omaha's main drag. But we weren't taking the main drag. This was a bus route, and it took us twice that long to get to school. We spent an hour and a half every day being hauled to and from a place we didn't want to be—a place that clearly didn't want us.

It's ironic they chose to bus us to Burke High. When the school opened in 1967, it was named for Harry A. Burke, who had been superintendent of Omaha Public Schools from 1946 to 1962. His tenure was tainted with allegations of racism. In a 2019 interview, North Omaha civil rights leader Harry Rhodes told the Nebraska State Historical Society that Burke "proclaimed that as long as he was superintendent, there would not be a Black educator in the school system, other than the two schools that served the Black community."[i] In 2020, David Bristow, editor of *History Nebraska*, told Omaha's Channel 3 News, "It was clear he (Burke) was only hiring Black teachers for the majority Black elementary schools in North Omaha. Omaha did not have a single Black high school teacher."

According to Bristow, Burke said his hiring practices reflected community sentiment in the 1950s and 60s. "I think there was an element of cowardice to it. As well as an element of actual preju-dice," Bristow said.[ii] The school still bears Burke's name.

We were not ready for the different world we'd find 120 blocks to the west, and Burke High was not equipped for the problems it was about to inherit. The gap in the income levels between the students bussed in and those who lived near the school was a mile wide, and it was obvious.

I am unsure where the idea originated to bus kids from a lower-income neighborhood to an upper-class neighborhood, but it put the school and staff on edge. It played a part in my behavior at school, and I never felt that I got treated like a student—like I belonged there. It seemed the teachers only tolerated us because they were forced to. They didn't want us at Burke, and we sure as hell didn't sign up to be there. I'd hear conversations about discrimination from the administration. I'd hear about upcoming events or things it seemed I should know about and realized I didn't get the same letters from the school other kids got, or if I did, I never saw them.

Gang culture was on the rise in the city and at school. I was still that wannabe, intrigued by gang culture, specifically gangs that didn't look so dirty. I can't say the same for my little brother. His whole crew was part of one of the gangs I didn't favor. Guys who carried themselves differently, had fresh fits, and didn't feel like they had to wear their gang on their sleeves or feel the need to advertise their affiliation intrigued me.

Back then, gangs in Omaha were about colors and flags. Ball caps were a big thing. Gangbanging was a lifestyle, and going after the opposing gang was a priority. If you wanted to gang bang to the extreme, you would wear a ball cap from the opposing set and, to be even more disrespectful, you'd take a piece of tape and place it across the logo on the ball cap. I watched all of this from the sidelines. I didn't get heavily involved with a gang until I got to prison, but I was very much a street-level wannabe.

Burke High was the gangbanging headquarters for a time. Three gang-related fights broke out in one day. I witnessed one that started when someone heard the principal saying, "We should've never let them into our schools." The Black student who overheard this comment responded with profanity. Word of what happened got around, and students planned a walkout. Rumors flew that gangs were going to show up and cause problems. Police established a menacing presence in front of the building. The local news was there interviewing kids. I took one look at the situation and decided that would be my last day at Burke High School.

And that's when the shit really hit the fan.

MY DAD WAS STILL BEATING me regularly at home. He had begun hitting much harder because I was no longer crying, and he didn't like it. I was done with being bussed to a school that could care less about me, and I was just as done crying from my dad's beatings or dealing with them at all, so I decided to run away from home. It wasn't a hard choice because I would rather deal with whatever came to me in the streets from strangers than what was happening to me at home from people who were my family and claimed to love me.

I knew of four other kids who lived in an abandoned house a few blocks from my parents, so that's where I went. The ringleader was a little older and knew a little more about street life and hustling than the rest of us. We were all living in an abandoned building and had to get creative to get the resources we needed. We would steal electricity and water from the elderly neighbor by running an extension cord from her outside outlet through our window. We would fill milk jugs with water from her outdoor faucet to wash up and flush the toilet in the house because we didn't have running water.

It was a trap house, but we didn't sell drugs; instead, we stole what we needed to get by. We broke into cars, usually in the Old Market in Omaha, because we knew that was where all the rich White people went to shop. The Old Market was our honey pot; we were like bees when it came to stealing from that area. Thinking back, the main reason we were stealing was because we were hungry. It was our way to survive and make sure we could eat. I feel bad looking back, but at the moment, stealing cars often silenced the stomach grumblings. As a teenager at that time, I'd say my decision-making skills were based on what we now call "being hangry."

One morning, while we were in downtown Omaha roaming the streets hungry, someone in our group pointed out the Hostess Factory, where they made Twinkies and bread. We went around to the back of the factory, took a big rock off the ground, and broke through a wooden garage door. We got into the building through the loading dock. Our leader left to get one of the cars we had stolen—a yellow Grenada hidden at one of our neighbor's houses. He returned with the car, and we filled it with snacks—bread, Twinkies, and Ho Ho's—then we drove off to the projects.

The projects were subsidized housing developments with low rent. In today's economy, it's called low-income housing. We didn't know it was low-income housing, and we didn't care. We were driving around the neighborhood in the projects, throwing boxes of snacks out the window to the kids. Before we knew it, we ran out. Turns out we didn't get enough, so we went back to the factory to get more.

This time, our curiosity got the best of us, and we went into the factory office. We found a set of keys, and it didn't take long to figure out which keys were for the Wonder Bread minivan. We lit up like lightbulbs. In no time, we filled industrial-size garbage cans with as many pastries and loaves of bread as possible and began loading the van. We left the factory and returned to the abandoned house, where we unloaded bread through the back door, throwing it into the basement. We didn't have a plan, but that didn't matter because stealing snacks hadn't been part of the plan for the day, and so far, so good. The one thing we knew for certain was that we wouldn't be hungry for quite some time.

All of this happened in the middle of the day. My brother came walking down the street while we were unloading, so I threw him a few Twinkies. He ate one and put the other in his pocket. It seemed like giving him those Twinkies was like sending out the bat signal for the police because shortly after he put that Twinkie in his pocket, the Omaha Police Department had us surrounded.

As the flashing lights and sirens converged, I had only one thought: Horace Mann Park. We had always said that if things ever went down, we'd scatter and meet later at the park. It was our safe zone. I sprinted away as fast as I could toward Horace Mann Park. I sat and waited, but nobody else showed up. I started to freak out, guessing everyone else must've been caught. When it was dark and I felt like the police probably weren't looking for me, I walked back to the neighborhood. They had the abandoned house taped off, and I saw their flashlights inside, searching. I couldn't go back to the house, so I asked two neighbor girls if I could crash on their couch. The very next day, we were watching the news at noon and saw a Crime Stopper report about the Wonder Bread heist. The news anchor said that if anyone has information leading to the apprehension of the people involved, they should contact the number listed on the screen. Again, it felt like the police got a bat signal because within half an hour, the cops were at the front door. My neighbors had snitched.

The police took me to the station and put me in an interview room. I sat alone in that room for at least two hours, and I remember seeing a camera in the corner. I don't understand why I was there for two hours before anyone came to talk to me, but I assume it was one of their tactics to make me uncomfortable. Finally, a police officer entered the room and told me to take off my shoes. What did my shoes have to do with anything? I thought I was there because of Twinkies and Ho Hos. Then it hit me, a few weeks prior, some people that I was staying with ran a credit card scheme and one of the older guys bought me a pair of Nikes—the exact shoes I was wearing at the police station and had been wearing at the bread factory. My friend only bought me those shoes because I didn't have any. This innocent gesture was about to become my new nightmare.

I took my shoe off, and the officer pulled out a plaster cast of a shoe print and compared the two.

"It's an exact match," he said. "Do you want to tell us what happened?"

If I knew one thing about street code, it was not to talk to the police. No matter their tricks or tactics, under no circumstance should I tell them anything. Officers came into the room and asked all types of questions. When I didn't respond, they did exactly what the streets told me they would and tried to tell me that my friends were already snitching on me. I didn't fall for that trick because I knew better. I knew they had all been taught the street code, but I wasn't sure if everyone was strong enough to abide by it under pressure. Turns out the odds weren't in my favor. The police caught my little brother with the Twinkie in his pocket, so it was off to juvie for me.

ANGER

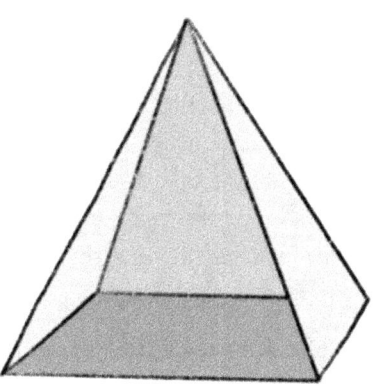

CHAPTER 10
AN ESSAY FROM THE JOURNALIST
WITH OLUSEYE

ONE OF KWAME GYAMFI'S foremost memories of growing up was in a neighborhood where everything was fast-paced as he searched for his identity in a conflicting world. You know those PG-rated movies with warnings of flashes, lights, and even provocative scenes of violence? That describes the environment Kwame, who was then known as Shannon, lived in during his formative years, and rather than being an observer of these events, he and other young lads like himself were participants in the anger, blood, and gangs that propelled their survival instincts. One would wonder what his story teaches or if the moral lesson is simple. His story tells how the formative years of a child can be marred by neglect and abuse. But how the story ends ... well, that's what makes the story worth telling.

Kwame's story tells of grass to grace, dregs to dignity. It was in North Omaha that he learned what it means to be a street kid—street smarts, agility, absconding from school and home—basically what a young lad needs to survive. For him, the street taunts him badly, even as it leaves indelible marks on his story. How can Kwame tell his story without these street experiences? How best can he tell his stories without this background, the truancy, the life he lived as an adult-child away from Mr. and Mrs. White, his adoptive parents, whose abuse (Mr. White) and complicity (Mrs. White) served as a propeller for his leaving home and living on the streets, in an abandoned house without electricity, water, or a couch to lay his head on, along with other kids caught in stories of their own.

When I met Kwame, these street stories were wrapped with concern. Every enunciated word carried a weight—the weight of a crying child caught within the labyrinth of a love-hate relation-ship. While his adoptive mother was loving, Kwame describes abuse at the hands of a father, who tripled his abusiveness when he became religious. While his mom would rub salve into his wounds after a beating, she seemed powerless or unwilling to intervene.

The backdrop for Kwame's story is a restless Midwest city in the 1980s and 90s. Racial tension was building in Omaha, and North Omaha was the epicenter. Malcolm X was born to Earl and Louise Little in 1925. The family lived at 3448 Pinkney Street (now Evans Street). Both Earl and Louise were active in the United Negro Improvement Association, which labeled them trouble-makers. After threats from the Ku Klux Klan, the Little family fled Omaha. By the time Kwame's family moved to 22nd and Sprague, just thirteen blocks from where the Littles had lived, the North Freeway had cut predominantly Black North Omaha in half. Heat in the neighborhood was rising from simmer to boil, and Kwame lived in the middle of it.

Kwame's story is a summation of the time, the city, and his home environment. Anger, blood, gangs, and survival. Looking at Kwame today, everyone who knew him by that name can imagine how he managed to survive. How the discipline and abuse applied by a military father both shaped and marred him, and how Kwame grew to champion the emancipation of African

American teenagers whose anger he recognizes. His mission now is to help the lonesome and angry kid avoid the school-to-prison pipeline that is the status quo for too many Black teens. I think this is just that simple: those who are greatly affected can truly help. And for this, Kwame Gyamfi remains a beacon, an authority in the story he tells, with the life he has lived and the one he is living now. So, you can say he was reborn and given a new name, but that is another story.

Kwame can recall the day his family moved from the house on 63rd Street to the house on 22nd and Sprague Streets. Moving day into the new neighborhood was a harbinger of the things he would experience in North Omaha. The first fight was never a coincidence, the parks where the gangs always gathered ushering him toward a life that would reflect him and affect him, irrespective of the morals supposedly instilled in his staunchly religious adoptive home. From my assessment, Kwame was a precocious child and a precocious teenager, courageous and unflinching with decisions that spurred him into a gang wannabe. Seemingly good virtues can be used negatively if they are not properly modeled. The world of gangs seeks those who are recalcitrant, who won't chicken out in the face of bullying or cower in the presence of the stocky, ripped young adults smoking on the corner in gang-dominated neighborhoods. Standing up to one of the members of a predominately Black gang was the beginning of the boys respecting Kwame. I could feel this in the tone of his voice retelling the story.

So, we see Kwame living out a story we've heard before: Abuse at home and early exposure to gangs, drugs, guns, sex, and theft. Kwame wasn't immune. He had his share, he paid the price, and he is living a corrective life. How would you explain the trajectory of his story, the story of a boy who doesn't remember living with his biological mom and was in the hands of very devout yet abusive adoptive parents? Kwame was caught in the web of searching for an identity with no real guide. He was without a positive role model who would relate to his experiences, someone who understood his struggles, and most importantly, someone who was Black.

The move to North Omaha also meant a new school, which required another form of survival. Kwame had to learn how to crack.

"I wasn't good at it. You must be witty to say it," he explained.

The imagery I have is those of rap battles when you say words like "Your mama is so (... blank ...), which is followed by a shit-ton of disparaging words that can make a weak heart cry. He needed those tools to survive the bus and the new school. But he had that innate survival instinct in him, now that I think of it. My mind flashed to the incident at the park where he protected his younger brother from gang bullies.

Add to that instinct Mr. White's investment in Kwame's self-defense—the gift of boxing gloves. For Mr. White, being a boxer himself, it was only appropriate to gift his children this sport that soon became a tool. The gloves aren't only a gift of self-defense but also a metaphor for Kwame to brace himself against the tumult he would persistently face at home and in the neighborhood.

"Just don't get beaten," his father would say.

And honestly, this is a subtle way to say don't be the one taking the last blow. Both in the new school and on the bus, life was a daily tussle for Kwame, and to survive, he must either crack or fight. The latter was the best tool for him.

Kwame's story has a ricochet or boomerang effect whenever he talks about his neighborhood in North Omaha. He spent most of his teenage years on the street, both literally and figuratively. The gangs were like pawns, Horace Mann Park like a chess board where all activities—the good, the bad, and the ugly—happened. This era in his life is an episodic frame on its own. As Kwame talked about these things, you can have flashes in your mind. Flashes and loud voices, snickering boys and girls, and sometimes, an older street brother standing afar trying to call the boys to order. And if you are patient to hear through these multiple voices, you can also hear the beating, pulsating hearts of the boys. The girls, who had come to eye their boys and watch the biceps and ripped bodies, shiver away in flight and fright. A young lad whose experience is solidified by these happenstances has no escape from a life that beckons imprisonment in the long run.

If you know Kwame as an adult, as he moves around in his still ripped, athletic body, you can tell that these were not muscles gained yesterday. Though he looks older, if you close your eyes, you teleport to a scene at Horace Mann Park. As I retell this, I fear for the young Kwame. How can you explain why he wasn't stabbed? The street is bloody, razz, and crazed, and you must be bloody, razzed, and crazed to survive. He tells stories of lost friends and acquaintances shot on porches or in parks. And God knows that it is never exaggerating to say that he might have seen bullets piercing through flesh or blades and knives ribbing tendons apart. The screech encapsulates his mind, solidifying his agility and reinforcing the importance of survival.

Being invisible was one thing young Kwame couldn't even do because of his socioeconomic situation at that time—rough hair, ripped and torn shoes. As an obnoxious teenager, the best response was to retaliate when faced with disparaging and condescending comments both from the pupils in his new school and on the bus ride to the school.

I see Kwame talk about these stories, and it is crystal clear that he who throws the finest blow is hailed and respected. As a gang wannabe, the park was his lab test. Remember when I said the gangs, the boys and girls in the neighborhood, are pawns? Yes, that should depict that to move from pawn to respected lord, you must earn it. His skills at throwing punches couldn't be hidden for long. The girls will smirk when he passes, and the boys will tell their brothers who are members of the gangs, who smoke and chill on their cars during the cool of the day and watch them play from afar. This stare is a haunting stare. A recruiting technique of knowing the boy who may not be a gang member but who they can rely on like their street child alibi, one who can scuttle inside the cloves as they peruse the field. And that is what Kwame soon became. He became a full man in a boy's body. A gangster by proxy. A torment by extension.

Kwame's life's story can't be balanced or fair without these North Omaha stories. These stories give a full hint as to why he does the things he does. Advocacy isn't borne of a thirst for fame but from pain, experience, and literally wearing the shoe and knowing where it pinches. The park was also where he had a front-row seat to violence; shootings like a movie, each scene flashing before his eyes. The realities of this experience forever etched in his mind. While Kwame spoke about it, his hands moved in rhythms that they hadn't before, gesticulating and trying all he could to recreate a one-man play of death.

Some things don't need much emotion or energy for one to feel the pangs and pain of it, and this is one of those things. The epoch of Kwame's life is marked like that. Imagine one who had to experience such at such an age; imagine the trauma, the stigma, and the fear. Imagine the voice that would have formed in their mind to brace up and defend themselves. In this case, it is a necessary evil. The highest of all forms of eroding fear is to witness death. Because after death, what's next? Imagine the courage that comes with fleeing through sporadic gunfire or running from a charging knife blade or machete. I wonder what again could move such a child. Homicide in the neighborhood was the straw that broke the camel's back for him and had a snowball effect on the entire neighborhood. It happened at Bronco Burgers. Rival gangs. A knife. A boy left dead.

Gang violence and racism took a toll on the way Kwame perceived school. School was a battle for him anyway and no longer provided much of an escape from the constant beatings at home. According to Kwame, he and his brother were getting hit, and when it was becoming unbearable, he had to leave. Hitting, it seemed, was the disciplinarian measure Mr. White knew best. Sadly, this discipline only changed Kwame's demeanor and attitude toward both home and school.

Mr. White did try to provide necessities for the boys, but it seemed to be done with the intention of scoring a point of provision. All through these earlier years, Kwame couldn't reconcile why the love professed by his adoptive father looked like something he had to earn. Yes, Mr. White did teach his boys to stand up for themselves, but his teachings were the reflection of some of his personal unanswered questions. Another lesson he taught them was the benefit of savings, even though Kwame and his brother thought that money might have been used to provide them with more than second-hand clothes. Without their father's knowledge, Kwame and his brother once took a bus downtown to the bank to withdraw their savings.

"It was like I had like eighty dollars, and he had like sixty," Kwame said. Well, you can guess what exuberant, youthful, and agile teenage boys will do with such money—they'll upgrade their wardrobes to compete with the boys in school and dress up. The brothers took their savings to the mall to buy new clothing and shoes, which they kept at their "cousin's" house. These cousins were peers living some blocks away, close but not related by blood. So, it was in their cousin's house that they changed into these new clothes before going to school.

This new endeavor made Kwame look cool and hot. New drips from Dickies, hoodies and all, and these appearances gave him an effulgence and set him up to realize what a boy could do with a little cash. Imagine how silly it would be to dress so well and without any money in one's pocket. His cousin showed him how to make money dealing pills, the available option to keep up with this new and expensive lifestyle beyond the watch of his adoptive parents.

Money and style are quick adolescent intoxicants. Aside from seemingly becoming the guy whose outlook and crack now commands respect, his swag, gait, and dress do the same. He carries himself differently at school, but that doesn't mean it gets easier. During his final year of middle school, glass broke, and a summer was ruined. I listened and imagined how a teenager who seemed to me moved from innocence to vulgarity could be influenced. This story isn't peculiar to him but could belong to anyone caught in the labyrinth of a dysfunctional environment.

"Tell us about the broken glass," I queried, adjusting my seat for another interesting recounting.

"It happened in the hallway," he began.

"So, I was walking in the hallway in the school building that had these big giant plexiglass style glass windows down the corridors."

"If you bang on the windows, you can make bass. *Boom! Boom! Boom! Boom!*" He continued, dramatizing the effect on an invisible wall, just like the way he banged on the corridor wall.

"So, I'm walking down the hallway. *Boom! Boom! Boom! Boom!* I can't remember who, but somebody was rapping with me, so we were out here climbing the hallways, and *boom!* One of the windows shattered. And the principal was right behind us."

Kwame spent the summer scraping gum and cleaning classrooms to pay for the busted window. I doubt if he ever told his parents about this. How could he when home was another tug of war? He had sworn to his brother that his form of defense to the beatings was to refuse to cry. This act infuriated his father even more. The beatings increased in intensity. This is the point in the story where Kwame leaves his parent's house to live in the abandoned house just a few blocks away.

While Kwame shares this part of his life—a period of three months marked by crime and survival—the classic novel *Lord of the Flies* comes to mind. Using this story that is familiar to many is the best way to create a mental picture of what the five boys had to go through for survival. While the classic novel was fictional and boys were on an island where they had to provide for their basic needs in every creative way, humanely and inhumanely, Kwame's exile and seclusion in this abandoned house was self-imposed, borne out of weariness with a home, where the abuse became intense.

Just like *Lord of the Flies*, there was an older boy in the house, the Ringleader. His election was democratic and ageist. He seemed to be the oldest of the four boys, so it was appropriate to crown him. He gave the orders and told the other boys what to do.

Before moving to the streets, Kwame's only crime was selling pills. Now, the boys had to find a way to eat, and most of their activities were motivated by basic human needs like hunger. "Since we had to fend for ourselves, we had to break into homes and cars, steal, and tap electricity just to live and keep warm."

Curious, I asked what Mr. and Mrs. White had done.

"Did they bother to look for you?"

He paused before answering.

"No, they didn't," he finally said.

"I guess it was because they knew where we were, which wasn't far from the house. They never called the cops to come get me. I think my dad knew that if he had called the cops, it would have been more of an issue for him."

His brother also knew where Kwame was, yet didn't join him in this self-imposed exit. He would stop by the abandoned house sometimes to say, "Hey."

Their basic means of survival was to steal electricity and water from the neighbors. They ran an extension cord through the window from the house of an old lady who lived next door to this house. A deep pan was turned into an electric skillet to boil water. They used the sink upstairs to wash up.

Downtown was their battleground. The Old Market in Omaha was where the rich people shopped, and it was easy, according to Kwame, to break into their cars. Stealing was the only way they knew to fill their empty bellies.

When they broke into the Hostess Factory, Ringleader went home to get a stolen car. They filled the yellow Grenada with snacks, bread, and Twinkies. And when the boys saw that they didn't get enough, they had to go back to get some more. They threw these Twinkies to kiddies they saw on the street. Even Kwame's brother benefited from the loot. It must have looked like a candy parade.

The boys' lair was soon invaded by the cops, who had been tipped off to the bread factory robbery. This is the first time Kwame mentioned being wanted or chased by the police. While I listened keenly, I saw the story take a different turn and tone. It is arguable that they did steal because they were hungry, but that didn't and wouldn't undermine the gravity of their offense, irrespective of their ages.

While they shared and munched on Twinkies, the cops ransacked their house. The boys staying in the house had made a pact to sprint to Horace Mann Park, where boys were turned into men should anything go down. The boys scattered like headless chickens. Kwame was the first to sprint to the park, and when he arrived, he was shook to discover that no one else was there. Worried about what might have happened, he ran back to the abandoned house to look for the other boys, but the police were already in the house, turning it down. He felt alone but, on the spot, re-strategized and found another place for cover in the house of two girls who lived nearby.

I do believe Kwame has always been a ladies' man, charming them with his presence, aura, charisma, and mostly his physique. The conclusion is not farfetched as I listened keenly to his stories, and in every part, a girl's name was mentioned. There is something about him that calls for ladies' softness toward him, and this is true with his story of succor for safety. He spent the night on the couch of these two sisters, only for them to turn him into the police the following day.

His arrest happened suddenly. That morning, before his arrest, he sat on the couch, still perplexed about the previous day's happenings and trying so hard to avoid conversation about why he was sleeping on the sofa at the sisters' house. They were magnanimous enough to let him in but also puzzled when he knocked on their door. His demeanor tells of something fishy, and this is confirmed when they turn on the TV and hear the news about the bread factory. One of the suspects was the boy now sitting on their couch. They clandestinely called the cops concerning

Kwame's whereabouts, and in a twinkle of an eye, like half an hour or less, the police pulled up to the house and apprehended him.

At the police precinct, Kwame was ushered to a small white room with a camera positioned at the corner. He was fourteen years old and had no parent, attorney, or other adult advocate. The hour he spent alone in that white room felt like two—two hours of silence, reflection, and fear of what might happen. He had displayed some toughness and cunning decisions hitherto, but the situation he now found himself in seemed to have outsmarted all the street smartness he had picked up at Horace Mann Park. The Ringleader had absconded and was nowhere to be found. Kwame's situation metamorphosized when the police matched a footprint found at the Hostess Factory to the pair of Nikes he was wearing. Those shoes were traced to a credit card scheme operated by an older guy who gave Kwame the shoes because the only pair he had was in rough shape.

The police asked Kwame to remove his shoe and then held it against a plaster cast of the print.

"Huh," one of the police said. "That's an exact match. Do you want to tell us what happened?"

Kwame knew the code of the street. He would not be the one to squeal, even when the cops told him they found his brother with Twinkies, and the other boys had confessed and fingered Kwame as the one who drove the stolen vehicle and masterminded the whole thing. Kwame knew this was a tactic to get suspects to talk. He wasn't falling for it. But at the end of the day, they had him for his part in the robbery and as an accomplice in the credit card scheme.

This opened a new chapter in Kwame's story as he ended up at the Douglas County Juvenile Assessment Center. His sentencing was witnessed by his parents, who sat on the bench behind him, his mother weeping. I wondered what would have been going on in their minds. Perhaps regret, perhaps a sense of shame, a sense of failing in their responsibility, having tried to raise him right and enforce discipline on him and his brother. I wonder if they knew how North Omaha, the house on 22nd and Sprague, and Horace Mann Park had formed Kwame. He internalized much of what he had experienced during those years, and he became angry. Crack, fight, and eventually flight became his tools for navigating and surviving this world of struggle.

Going to the juvey meant he became separated from his adoptive parents. He was angry; they were too. At one point during the sentencing, Judge Colleen Buckley confronted Mr. and Mrs. White and ordered them to go to parenting class. Hearing this, Mr. White bellowed, "I don't need parenting classes. I know what I'm doing. I know how to raise 'em. I raise them according to the Bible."

Seeing the objection, Judge Buckley said, "Well, you either go to parenting classes or I'm going to put you in jail for thirty days."

Kwame had never seen anyone talk to his father like that.

Kwame's anger was rooted in the fact that his adoptive parents neglected him. He cannot recount one happy memory with his father. You can tell that Kwame was an angry child with all these said and unsaid experiences. He was always looking for any avenue to detonate. Kwame carried this anger into the system. He constantly got into fights with other boys at the two foster houses where he was placed and was eventually kicked out.

"I would blank out sometimes when I would get upset," he recalls. "I would just blank out and it didn't matter who was there, I was trying to fight with you."

A grown man now in his fifties—the man once known as Shannon White—takes responsibility for that young man's actions in North Omaha. Yet, something innately called him to rebel against the odds of Black teens exposed to abuse, anger, crime, and gangs. He has become what Bayard Rustin calls an "angelic troublemaker," informed by his experiences at 22nd and Sprague Streets.

CHAOS

ELEVEN
WITH LASHAWNDA

THE JUVENILE DETENTION center was called the Youth Center at the time, and this would be my first time in court. My mom and dad were seated on the benches behind me, and I was at the table with my representative. The court was trying to put me in a foster home, and when they finally succeeded, it was like heating water, watching it boil, and waiting until it spilled over. I was a very angry child at the time. I got kicked out of the Youth Emergency Services (YES) house and Nebraska Children's Home for fighting because I let my temper get the best of me.

Most of the time, I felt like people were picking on me, and my way of dealing with it was fighting. I didn't care how big or small the issue, I was going to fight. If you lied and it involved me, slighted me, or so much as looked at me the wrong way, I was ready to fight. I really didn't understand my emotions. I can say now that I had a lot of misplaced anger, which played out in my behavior. I was a kid who didn't know who I was, and after getting beatings at home for so many years, I normalized fighting. It became a way of life. As an adult, I know anger is a very complex emotion, but I didn't know that as a kid. I know I wasn't angry at the kids I was fighting; I was angry at the fact that I had two parents who were supposed to love me and even went out of their way to adopt me, only to abuse me.

I repeatedly questioned the reason people would go out of their way to be abusive to children, trying to make some sense of it all when the truth is there was no justification for the actions of my father and the silence of my mother, but that doesn't change the fact that it was fucked up. It felt like I was the one being penalized. I never even had a birthday party growing up. My first birthday party wasn't until I turned forty-one. I could count on one hand the number of happy times I had with my father because the majority of our moments together were him trying to beat something out of me physically. I can't speak to the state of mind of my father when it comes to the beatings. It just became routine, so I expected a beating just like you would expect dinner. I remember the judge told my dad he had to go to parenting classes or she was going to put him in jail for thirty days. He told the judge that he didn't need parenting classes. He told her that he raised us according to the Bible, not the law or any other shit. It's always interesting when people interpret the Bible in their own way and use it to excuse their behaviors. I had never heard or seen anybody talk to my parents the way this judge talked to them. I remember thinking she was not playing, and I will never forget her name: Judge Buckley.

When I got kicked out of the Nebraska Children's Home, Judge Buckley gave me two options. She told me I could go to Kearney, Nebraska, to the Youth Rehabilitation and Treatment Center until I turned eighteen, or I could go to Boys Town in Omaha. The court officers took me to a room and showed me a video about Boys Town. Was somebody playing a joke on me? Boys Town didn't look like a juvenile center, jail, or detention center, at least not the ones I was familiar with. I chose Boys Town.

Boys Town looked like Camp Cupcake, as far as I was concerned. Judge Buckley gave me three rules to follow: I couldn't wear gang colors, I couldn't run away, and I couldn't get into fights. I didn't have a problem with the inability to wear gang colors or running away. Those rules were the least of my worries, but when she said no fighting, it was as if the world had stopped. I mean, at that time, if you looked up the word fight, it probably had a picture of me next to it. I needed her to elaborate on what exactly she considered a fight. I knew I had to make some changes because Judge Buckley wasn't someone I cared to disregard. She made it clear that if I broke any of those rules, she would send me to Kearney until I turned eighteen. Judge Buckley meant business, so I knew she was not issuing an empty threat. If I screwed up this opportunity, she wouldn't have any problem sending me to Kearney until I was eighteen. And it wasn't a decision that she would lose any sleep over. I knew I was on her turf, and she repped her judicial set well. The last thing I needed to be was her opp.

I struggled the first year at Boys Town. It was tough. I was trying to get my mind settled, but I was hostile. I was angry. I also struggled academically because I never connected with the material or the teachers. I always needed an explanation for things. For example, the teachers would give me an assignment, but I needed to know why I needed to complete it, like what benefit it would have for me. I had not had positive experiences when it came to education, and I had not had many teachers who cared enough about me to spend time to show me the benefits of school. It was very difficult for me to see the point of most of the stuff at school because I knew people who went to college and did very well in school and ended up back in the hood. I knew people with full-ride scholarships and saw them return to the hood, so I needed proof and some buy-in as to why I should put any effort into academics. I needed an explanation regarding getting all the accolades and being able to leave the hood because of academics, only to return and struggle. It didn't make sense to me, and there wasn't ever a good enough explanation to make me want to value education.

I didn't know that some of the things from my upbringing at home were gonna be beneficial to me at Boys Town. I came from a very strict household, a military household. Before I got to Boys Town, I would say I was in my feral period. I was on the streets and getting into unnecessary trouble, which is the reason I got involved in the juvenile justice system, court, foster care, and Boys Town. It was my poor decisions that got me kicked out of different placements and, to be honest, my mind was all over the place. So, it took a minute before I could get settled at Boys Town. There were moments that made things easier, and there were challenges. The relationships that I had with the other kids helped. I made a good friend who became my boy, my guy, my right-hand man. He helped to keep me grounded, even though he got kicked out of Boys Town.

I can't talk about my time at Boys Town without mentioning the behavior model they follow. There is a definite process and protocol for behaviors. Boys Town used a point card system. It's different now, but when I attended, you were given a card, and when you followed expectations or did anything positive, you would write it down, and staff would sign off on it. Then, at the end of the day, staff sat down with you to add up all your cards. If you had more positive points, you got your privileges for the next day. However, if you had more negative points, you were placed on what is called a sub. Sub is a punishment system that you must complete by doing chores, correcting behavior, and having positive interactions with staff to earn your privileges back. So, for example, a staff member says to you, "Hey, can you take the trash out?" And your response is, "I'm busy. I am not trying to take the trash out right now." The staff member might say, "I understand how you feel. But I really would appreciate it, and it helps keep the house flowing, if I could get you to take the trash out right now." You continue to say, "No, I'm not going to do that," and that staff member will say, "Okay. I want you to give yourself a negative 500 points for not following instructions and not doing the task immediately." And you get your card out and write -500. Boys Town was definitely going to hold you accountable.

Now, you can guess when you're just getting to Boys Town, your attitude is, "I ain't doing none of that. Fuck you and fuck this card." In this instance, staff would implement the five-second rule. At this point, all the kids in the house must go to their rooms, and you are considered intensive. The staff would say you're under intensive right now, and you automatically lost privileges for a period of time. We quickly learned there was nowhere to go but downhill when they called the five-second rule. When you had a kid like me, staff calling the five-second rule would just piss me off more because, at that point, I felt like I had nothing to lose. My thought process was if I was going to lose privileges anyway, then fuck it. I was gonna tear some shit up, break furniture, and punch holes in the wall. I might as well give it my all. If I had to describe my behavior during a five-second rule, it would be like the song by Miley Cyrus: I was a wrecking ball.

The living arrangements at Boys Town were different as well. Family teachers, usually a married couple, were in charge of each house, and these were nice, family-style houses, the nicest I'd ever been in. Some family teachers and some assistant family teachers were easier than others. Some of them understood the struggles of most of the kids that resided at Boys Town, and they tried to make it easy for you. When I say easy, I mean something as simple as asking you to pass them the remote so you could earn some points because you followed basic instructions. Those points added up quickly, so it made a difference. It helped to have a few people who would bend the rules a little in your favor, especially given the circumstances. If you wanna give me five hundred points for passing you the remote, I'm not going to argue about it. They would try to find anything positive that you did to help you get your points back so that you could gain back your privileges.

You had to clean the house when you were on sub from a five-second rule. These very nice houses we lived in had to be cleaned with great detail. You'd have to vacuum and dust the edges of the floorboards. When you were done cleaning, they would inspect your work thoroughly. I was used to inspections after cleaning because, growing up in my military house, my father inspected everything. When I did the dishes, he would come into the kitchen and inspect every single plate, and if they didn't meet his standard of cleanliness, my brother and I had to do twenty-five push-ups per dish. Trust me, I understood cleanliness and I understood what it meant to pay attention to details, but as a kid, I didn't know that those were skills I would need. I think it's interesting that although my dad was a strict and harsh man, he taught me some important skills for life. He just had a fucked-up way of going about it.

My first family teachers were a White couple from Louisiana, and I couldn't stand the wife. She was very southern and had a thick accent, but what I hated the most was that she called us "BOY." I'm not going to give a history lesson about the term; just know it wasn't from a place of respect. I felt uncomfortable around her, and I did not trust her. I was happy when I found out they decided to leave Boys Town. I enjoyed the family dynamic of Boys Town. I had a roommate from the Bahamas. We would always get boys from the Bahamas, which I always wondered about because who would choose to leave the Bahamas to come to Omaha? It turns out that Boys Town had a satellite deal in the Bahamas, so we had a lot of kids from there.

In my second year at Boys Town, I started to get my shit together. I was doing so well that I became an unofficial leader in the house. I know, I know what you're thinking. It may be difficult to imagine me as a leader of anything with the temper that I had, and shit, I couldn't believe it either. But there I was, taking advantage of this time at Boys Town and choosing to make the best of it. I was experiencing something new; I realized I felt safe there. I can't remember ever experiencing that sense of security before.

I became a mentor to a ten-year-old kid in the house. I don't think becoming his mentor was originally a part of the plan, but the Boys Town staff noticed the kind of relationship I had built with the kid. This kid was a handful, especially when he would have a five-second rule called on him and had to go intensive. He would grab snacks, run out of the house, and climb a tree. It was annoying because we could be in the middle of getting ready to go on a field trip, and if he flipped out and we went into a five-second rule, we would have to drop everything and go to our rooms. I mean, everything stopped. It was a roller coaster all the time when dealing with this kid—a cruel game of red light, green light, which was exhausting for everybody. He would sit in the tree, eating his snacks and refusing to come down. Staff would try to talk him down, but I was the one who would climb the tree and get him to go back into the house with me. I liked having some leadership at the house because it meant I was doing well, and Judge Buckley wouldn't have to make good on her threats.

The vacancy for family teachers for my house was eventually filled. The Crawfords were amazing people who had a huge impact on my life. I still keep in touch with their family. Mr. Crawford was an ex-Major League Baseball player and sports back to me.

My dad had introduced me to boxing, and I played youth football for three years in North Omaha. I loved it, but it came with turmoil. My dad would sit in his car and watch me and my brother practice. Sometimes, when he'd been drinking, he'd get disruptive and confront the coach about the way he was treating us. One day, things escalated, and my dad pulled a knife. That was the end of youth sports for me outside of the boxing gym.

One of the treasures of North Omaha is the CW Boxing Club. Carl Washington opened the gym in 1978, and it grew into a youth resource center. Washington discovered boxing as an outlet for his rage after his nephew was killed by police during civil unrest in the neighborhood in 1968. For decades, Washington has offered kids in North Omaha a door that is always open as long as they follow his rules. I found my way there off and on over my years in Omaha. In the 1990s, a seven-year-old neighborhood kid named Terrance Crawford started hanging around CWs, just like his father, uncle, and grandfather had. Terrance "Bud" Crawford won his first world boxing championship in 2014.

When Mr. Crawford (my new family teacher at Boys Town, not Bud) asked, "Why don't you start playing sports?" It was as if somebody had unlocked a forgotten door inside me. I began playing football, basketball, and running track at Boys Town. Football was the perfect outlet for me, especially my temper. Then you add that it's a sport where it's a part of the game to hit people and be physical. It turned out to be exactly what I needed. Sports changed everything because I didn't want to miss any practices, track meets, or games. I knew that for me to be able to play, I had to do well academically. Now academics made sense to me. I was able to view school through a different lens. I became aware that I could play sports and, if I did well, possibly make them a career. I made sure that I completed all my schoolwork and homework every day, so sports ultimately motivated me to succeed in academics. I even did a little better in math, which was the bane of my existence in school.

CHAPTER
TWELVE
WITH LASHAWNDA AND CINDY

THE LEGACY of Boys Town sports runs deep. When Monsignor Nicholas Wegner became the director of Boys Town in 1948, he brought with him a vision for using the discipline and training of athletics to give the boys (it was all boys until 1978) a positive focus and something to take pride in.

Wegner financed his seminary education by pitching semi-pro baseball. He declined contract offers from the Chicago Cubs and St. Louis Cardinals to follow his religious calling. Still, he understood the power of sports to help build character and promote the home and its mission. Wegner oversaw the golden era of Boys Town Cowboy sports in the 1950s and 60s. In those glory days, the Cowboys won sixteen state titles in various sports and garnered nationwide attention. The 1963 football team was undefeated and nationally ranked.

It was different back then. More than 900 boys lived in dormitories, and the goal was to give every single one of them an opportunity to participate in sports at some level. Things changed in the 70s and 80s. Family homes replaced dorms, and girls were now on campus. The Boys Town population went from 900 to less than 300, and kids didn't stay around as long.

Still, sports were a big deal when I was at Boys Town from 1990 to 1992. Former NFL receiver and Olympic sprinter Lawrence Burton and his wife Ida were family teachers in one of the other houses. *Sports Illustrated*, back when it was the word in sports, wrote a cool article about Burton and his post-NFL life at Boys Town. One of the photos with the article shows Boys Town founder Father Edward J. Flanagan and some of his boys with Lou Gehrig and Babe Ruth. It was October 1927. The Yankees had just won the World Series. In July 1990, Michael Jordon was in Omaha to receive the Father Flanagan Award for Service to Youth. I got to shake his hand and noticed that his suit was rumpled. Yeah, sports were a big deal at Boys Town, and I was just catching on.

Sports gave me a reason—a reason to do well in class (or at least marginally better in math) and a reason to keep my points up in the house. I wanted to compete, and now that I had focus and motivation, I was all in. Football. Basketball. Track. Sports changed the way I looked at what was possible in my future. I had never realized I was that fast. Then I saw. Oh, I'm fast. And I'm strong. It was an affirmation that I had more to offer.

Kids came to Boys Town from across the country and beyond, but we were all from the hood. Some of us sounded different, but we all had pretty much the same thing in common: We had fucked-up childhoods, one way or the other, and we were just trying to figure out how to navigate that. It created this special sense of camaraderie. And that carried over to sports, where my class was excellent.

I was never the greatest basketball player. I made the team, but I was a bench warmer. Football was where I shined. My football coach at Boys Town was Bob Nizzi. Later, he'd have a grand-daughter you may have heard of: Caitlin Clark. In 1990, we made it to the state football playoffs for the first time in seven years.

Our first playoff game was against Nebraska City. We won a thriller 29-28. The next week, luck wasn't on our side, and we lost 14-15 to Mt. Michael.

Our across-town rival was Father Flanagan High School. Yes, it was named after the founder of Boys Town. Flanagan High was built in North Omaha in 1982 for non-traditional students. It closed in 1997, but while I was at Boys Town, all the project dudes went to Flanagan. We had so many fights on the football field that coaches wouldn't let us take our helmets off until we were back on the bus. Flanagan did have phenomenal athletes, and it was a fun rivalry.

Sports also showed me another side of Nebraska. North Omaha, where I grew up, is only six square miles of a state that covers almost 77,000 square miles. You can live in North Omaha and be isolated. Later, I'd learn that once I left North Omaha, my odds of getting pulled over tripled. But before I got to Boys Town, I hadn't spent much time away from the hood. Now, I was traveling to football and basketball games across the Missouri River to Council Bluffs, Iowa, and to small Nebraska towns like Fremont, Columbus, and David City.

One night after a basketball game in Columbus, Nebraska, we stopped at KFC for something to eat. We were sitting there eating when a little White girl walked up. She probably was no more than three or four years old. She walked up to our table and rubbed my hand. Her mom rushed over and said, "I'm so sorry. She's never seen a Black person before." Like Dorothy in *The Wizard of Oz,* that's when I knew I wasn't in Kansas anymore.

I learned about racism in Nebraska just by playing football at Boys Town. To play other schools our size, we traveled to small towns and Catholic high schools. Everywhere we went, we were getting "N-this, N-that." I mean, I learned stuff I never even knew was racist. I never heard as much racism as I did on the football field. One game, it got so bad that we complained to our coach.

"Hey man, they out here talking crazy to us."

Coach looked at us and said, "Well, you are playing football. Just go knock them down." So, we went and beat the piss out of that team. When we knew certain teams were going to be racist, we were extra motivated for those games.

Sports and discipline were not the only focus at Boys Town. The program was well-rounded when it came to meeting the needs of the youth it served. I particularly loved the barbering program. Back home, I used to cut hair, my own, as well as my brother's, and then kids in the neighborhood. When I was only fourteen, I was shaving Jordan symbols and Nike swoops in people's hair.

My decision to begin cutting hair stemmed from a haircut nightmare. My dad used to cut my hair and did a terrible job. One day, he cut my hair, and it was a disaster. I got upset, so he gave me the clippers and told me to cut my own hair. I did and taught myself to cut hair from that point on. Thanks, Dad, for allowing me to show you how to turn lemons into lemonade. I knew he was expecting failure when he handed me those clippers. I'm sure it pissed him off when it backfired, and I loved every minute of it.

The decision to get involved with the barbering program was an easy choice. When I left Boys Town, I went to barber school to get the rest of the credits I needed to be a licensed barber, but I never finished. My father eventually got over his bitterness at my success with the clippers and was excited about me becoming a barber. At one point, he entertained the idea of potentially opening a barber shop in Omaha, but unfortunately, it never happened.

There was a sense of camaraderie at Boys Town. The kids there shared the same stories and had suffered similar traumas and struggles in life. We all grew up in rough areas despite where we lived, from the Bahamas to Nebraska. I am grateful for the experience at Boys Town and for the Crawfords. Boys Town was a bittersweet experience that I will never forget. I say it was bittersweet because I had good times, but some low points will stick with me as well.

I had a roommate I was extremely close with. He was an All-State wrestler. A girl wrote him a note asking him to sneak to the girl's dorm and bring me along because her friend had a crush on me. I had no interest in entertaining Boys Town girls. As far as I was concerned, they were at Boys Town because they had issues, too, so hell no. We were in the same boat, which didn't interest me then. I told my friend he shouldn't go, but of course he went anyway. The girl got mad because I didn't show up with him and she snitched on him the next day. He lost his scholarship offers and ultimately moved back to his hometown of Chicago. Unfortunately, a few years later, I found out he was shot and killed. I was so angry at those girls and really hated that girl who snitched on him after that incident. I was so hurt. It felt like leaving Boys Town changed the trajectory of his life.

Boys Town also changed the trajectory of my life. I had begun to focus and sharpen my talents in football. I was a decent player and was getting recruiting attention from several schools. Boys Town was not supportive because I wasn't interested in the schools they wanted me to attend. But the Crawfords were 100 percent supportive of wherever I wanted to go. They went with me on school visits, which I believe cost them their jobs at Boys Town. When we returned from one of the school visits, the Boys Town administration came to the house and pulled the Crawfords outside for a conversation, which ended with them leaving and me being devastated.

I'm proud of Boys Town and what they did for me and continue to do for youth today. I regret that when I left, they didn't have the programs to follow up with and support graduates. Our class had a high mortality rate from violence, and many of us, like me, ended up in the system. Still, the connections I made through Boys Town have shaped my life. When I graduated, my class was only seventy-two people. Although that's not a large number, these were kids who had become my extended family. I count other alumni as mentors and lifelong friends. Boys Town challenged me to be better and want better for myself, and I left there with a different perspective on life.

TOP: Boys Town Class of 1992

CENTER: Prom night

CENTER: Playing pool while the children of my family teacher looked on.

BOYS TOWN

BOTTOM: Relaxing on a summer Boys Town getaway.

DISCONTENT

THE SUMMER after I graduated from Boys Town, I broke my ankle in a pickup basketball game. I was dunking and heard it pop. My brother carried me back to my parents' house. This was a setback. Some small schools had recruited me to play football. I had chosen the Western Washington Vikings, an NAIA school with a pretty good football team. What really attracted me to Bellingham were my former family teachers, the Crawfords. They had moved to Washington when they left Boys Town. I stayed in contact with them, and they helped me move to Bellingham and get enrolled in community college while I rehabbed my ankle and worked on fulfilling some academic requirements. I was focused on joining the Vikings as a wide receiver as soon as possible. Rob Crawford worked out with me and threw me passes while I practiced my route running.

Bellingham was different from Nebraska in so many ways. It was lush and beautiful. I'd never seen trees like that before. Where I was from, it was just city trees—it was never trees everywhere. In Bellingham, you could drive around a corner, and it opens to some mountain ridge that looks crazy. The ocean and Puget Sound were right there! I was staying with the Crawford family in their ranch-style house in the country. Every morning, I would go running and see Mount Baker, this huge snow-capped mountain, in the background. It was awe-inspiring. When you're not used to seeing any of these things, it broadens your perspective. The sense of safety I'd found at Boys Town stayed with me in Bellingham. The people were different. I didn't sense the darkness I'd felt in North Omaha. I didn't experience racism.

You can learn a lot about a new city by visiting the mall. I would wander the mall in Bellingham, checking out the kind of stores they had, chatting with business owners, and observing people. It's where I listened and learned about the culture, where to eat, what clubs were hot. It's also where I got some part-time work at a clothing store and some modeling gigs. I always have liked fine clothes.

The first day I was at Western Washington, they had the Red Square dance, which was this annual back-to-school gathering with bands and DJs. Now, this was my first exposure to college and to a whole different environment. They assigned me a tour guide, and the two things I remember most were seeing people in little boats out in the water watching the whales. What was wrong with those people? A whale could put a tail up and tip them little bitty old boats over. Then, at the dance, I heard some people yelling, and I turned around and saw a male and a female rappelling off the admin building naked. When they reached the ground, they got on mountain bikes and rode off. I wasn't in Nebraska anymore.

I worked out at the Western Washington facilities, but it was up to me to figure out how to rehab my ankle. This was 1992, and there weren't any internet or YouTube videos to help you understand how to rehab a broken bone. So even though I was working hard, I couldn't plant my foot on the out cut. As a receiver, you have to be able to run the out route. I could run every other route, but when I went to plant my right foot and push off to run the out route, it would always hitch me up. It took me a long time before I was able to regain that. In the meantime, I went to community college, took basic classes, made friends, and fell in love.

I met another guy who was also rehabbing, trying to get back into football shape. He was from Canada and became one of my best friends in Washington. Bellingham is about fourteen miles from the Canadian border. I couldn't afford to return to Nebraska for holidays and breaks, so he would take me to his parents' cabin in the Surrey Valley near Vancouver. It was gorgeous. Every time I would go to their house, I would fall asleep because it was so cozy. They had a fireplace in the middle, and it was warm, comfortable, and safe.

My buddy was more successful in his rehab and later had the opportunity to try out for the Seattle Seahawks. He made the Seahawk's practice squad but then got seriously injured in practice, and they had to life-flight him out of the stadium.

While I was rehabbing, I also had to take math classes to make up some academic deficiencies. Algebra. I couldn't see the relevance of algebra to my life other than a hoop I had to jump through so I could play football. It was a struggle. I'd go to class early, sit in front, pay attention, and still bomb my tests. I can look back now and see the value in the struggle, in working hard at something just to be competent. I learned it's okay not to be great at everything.

While I was at Whatcom Community College struggling through math, I met a girl. It was like one of those love-at-first-sight kind of deals. We fell fast, and we fell hard. We were together so much we became a campus joke. If you saw me, then you would see her. Or if you saw her, you know I was right around the corner somewhere. I would say that was the first time I was really in love where I was goo goo ga ga for somebody.

Our schoolwork suffered, and I lost my focus. Eventually, I gave up on playing college football because I was just tired of dealing with the pain and all this other stuff. I just was done with it.

My girlfriend was an Iranian immigrant. Her family was Bhá'í, which is a group of people who had been persecuted and ostracized in Iran. They were granted asylum in the United States. Her father was a doctor, and they didn't know she was dating an African American. It was a few months in before I went over to their house, and they found out who I was.

By this time, I had pretty much stopped going to school. I had two jobs. I was DJing at a small club in Bellingham called Club USA. The main DJ was from Canada, and he would sometimes be late. When I first started going to Club USA, all I did was listen to the music. I have always loved music, and Bellingham had a used record store where I was always finding old hip-hop vinyl. One day, the DJ said, "I'm struggling to get here on time. Do you want to open for me? Do an opening set when the club opens?" Heck yeah.

So, I spun the Electric Groove Hour from eight to nine. I was DJ Catfish, and I would curate different types of music they weren't listening to up in that part of the country. They were listening to a lot of West Coast, a lot of techno. I was playing a lot of East Coast and house music. It was a different vibe; some people started to show up to listen to what I was playing. They came early just to hear the different music, and I loved that, even if I didn't get paid a whole lot.

I also worked at Ross Dress for Less, hanging clothes on racks, which helped pay the bills. That's when my girlfriend got pregnant. When she told me, I was prepared. I was ecstatic. I wasn't afraid. All I thought about was that I needed to make more money to take care of my girl and my baby. But that's not what happened.

Without ever talking to me, she decided to end the pregnancy. At the time, abortion was illegal in the state of Washington. She and her friend and a family member drove down to California. And that was that.

I couldn't get ahold of her. Remember we were always together, and now I can't reach her. I was frantic. Finally, one of her friends called me and told me what happened, and I was distraught. Nobody had ever brought abortion up to me before that. It was never a thing. I had never been in a situation where a girl had gotten pregnant, and I never even knew anybody who was in a situation like that. It was all new for me, and it was a surprise. I didn't understand why she did it.

I never got it until I called her house one day. Her father answered the phone and told me that his daughter was not going to marry an African American. He told me I could never see her again and asked me to stop calling.

That wasn't the first time I heard something like that, but it struck a chord because I had met these people. I had met them, and they knew me and their daughter were head over heels for each other. They pretty much killed that dream and broke something within me.

My rehab buddy from Canada stuck with me and tried to get me out of my funk. He tried to get me out of the house and finally convinced me to take a road trip to Canada. Driving back at two in the morning, we had the radio on and heard the world premiere of Whitney Houston's *I Will Always Love You*. Whitney started singing, and I started bawling. My buddy pulled over to the side of the road and hugged me while I cried.

I put up a shield for a long time after that. In my mind, I was an innocent until then—we were both innocents—and that just killed the innocence. I never felt the same after that.

I left Bellingham broke and broken. I cried as the Greyhound bus left the lush Pacific Northwest and headed toward the vast plains, my mix tape the soundtrack to my failure. I wasn't making enough money to sustain living up there. It was more expensive than Nebraska, so I ended up right back in North Omaha. Everybody knew I went away for college, for football. I was getting out. I was gone for almost two years. Now, everyone wanted to know what happened.

It didn't work out. I'm back here with ch'all fools on the block again.

BACK BEFORE JUVIE and Boys Town and Bellingham, back when I was first finding my way around North Omaha, I was with the wannabes, and we all looked up to the OGs around us. We watched those older dudes on the courts, playing streetball with the same aggression that drove them through life in such a place. We talked how they talked, moved how they moved. They noticed us eventually and put us to work. After a while, they let us join them on the courts. I loved hoopin'.

Now I was back, and I was one of the older dudes. At first, I tried to go legit. I was living in the basement of the house at 22nd and Sprague. My parents had moved to Michigan and rented the house to someone else. They decided I could rent the basement. It was sparse—a bathroom with a shower and a small bedroom but no kitchen. I didn't know what to do. I was doing odd jobs like making Gyros at a kiosk down at the bus station. I tried to get jobs outside of North Omaha, and every time I did, I'd get pulled over. I had a '77 Chevy Impala, brown with a light town top. It was a North Omaha car, and it felt like every time I left the hood, I got pulled over. I was just trying to get to work! I lost my job at a telemarketing company in West Omaha because I was late for work three times in my first two weeks. Yep. I got pulled over three times.

My next job was washing windows for a company in Millard, which is also on the west side of Omaha. I was driving to work one morning when my car broke down at 132nd and Q Streets. It was 8:00 a.m. in the middle of rush hour traffic. I was in the turn lane when my car stalled. I tried to push my car around the corner into a Sinclair service station, but nobody stopped to help me.

I finally got the car into the service station lot. I walked into the Sinclair. There were attendants at two counters, and they both ignored me. This was a *service* station. My car was broken down in their lot. *Oh shit. It was one of those places.*

I went outside to the pay phone and called my boss. He was a big White guy, but he was cool with me, and he was fair. I told him I was at the Sinclair, and my car was stalled. He drove his window-washing truck to the station and parked in front of my car. We had the hood up and were trying to figure out what was wrong. It looked like the alternator was the culprit.

Two mechanics walked toward us from the service station. They told us we had to move our vehicles. My boss looked at them and said, "Well, as you can see, the car is stalled."

"Doesn't matter," one mechanic said. "You gotta get that car out of here. Now!"

One of the guys had a screwdriver in his hands, and I could tell my boss was picking up on the vibe. Remember that I'm one of those hood kids, so I know what the action is all about. My boss went back to his truck and grabbed his big monkey wrench.

"You're a *service station,* but you're not gonna help us, are you?" He looked at them for a long time. I was thinking, he's a big dude, and if he hits one of them, it's gonna be a problem. He walked slowly back to his truck and grabbed a tie line to tow my car.

My boss towed my car to his house. He canceled our window cleaning jobs for the day and took me to the parts store. We got the car running, but I was done with trying to work outside the hood. I decided to stick to North Omaha.

KWAME: The next chapters of my life are no Hallmark movie. Things go dark, really dark, for a few years. I asked the fiction writer to hear my story and then tell it how he saw it.

NOW, I was truly back. I stood on the corner with a rag over the long, twisted braids on my head, slingin' in the hot sun. Being on the outskirts of their neighborhood, the gangs never bothered me about what color I had on. I had to do what I had to do to get a dollar or two. I pushed weed mostly, sometimes dope. I'd seen guns—probably more than my father—women, and barrels of cocaine bought and sold on the daily. Everybody had their vice, and the fiends and OGs knew I was dependable and that I'd keep my mouth shut. But not everyone was like me, and the police had been gliding through our hood like I used to glide the river on that sailboat in Virginia. They scoped the streets, just waiting to snatch us up from the jungle and throw us into the zoo. Locked bars and armed guards were a future we all could see.

"You hear what went down?" One of the little homies from down the block. He was a gang banger from Chicago; before that, he'd put in work on the East Coast.

"What's that?"

"They all got indicted. All the OGs. They all gone. 5-0 came in the night, no-knock warrants. Somebody talked."

"Who?" This was bad.

"I don't know. Someone tryin' to save they own ass."

The beat of my heart quickened. The hair on my neck stood. I felt for what I had in my pockets—enough left to get cold cuffs on my wrists—looked around for flashing lights. Maybe someone talked about me, too.

"I guess you're that dude now."

"What do you mean?"

"You just graduated, cuz. You're an OG now."

"Shit, I've always been an OG." I played it cool. "'Bout time you recognize."

The homie laughed. "So, what are we gonna do?"

I didn't have an answer then, but I developed one quickly enough. You stop moving on the streets, you drown.

I had some t-shirts made declaring my allegiance when all I ever was on the streets was a wannabe. Block letters across the chest. Reppin' before I was even blessed in. I claimed the gang that ran under the radar—didn't waste time taggin' up the block; all about the money. I eventually had the words branded on my chest.

I TURNED TO ROBBERY AFTER SLINGIN', but I only took from other dudes on the street, fiends and other criminals who probably stole what I was stealing. Money, watches, jewelry —shit that I could use or offload quickly. And it paid, too. I always had fresh gear, new kicks, and clothes—Chuck Taylors and Dickies were my style. I had a reputation, people looking up to me when the ones ahead of me got locked up. But I never forgot my mother telling me to do something with my brain.

When things got hot, or when I just needed to get the hell out of that life for a minute, I went to the movie theater out west to catch a matinee alone. I especially enjoyed the double features. Other times, I'd go to the library downtown to read. And I'd spend entire days devouring the books I'd find. I wanted to know more about my African heritage, so that section of the stacks called to me. Most Black folks can only see as far back as their grandparents on their family trees, and some not even that far. And, like me, some didn't even know their biological fathers or what name they were born with. It's a terrible thing not knowing what you were called before the system gave you a name. It's terrible still when the name that system gives you comes hand in hand with bruises and broken homes.

THE STREETS WERE WEARING on me. I needed out so I enrolled in Job Corps in the Pine Ridge area of Nebraska. I thought it might look like Bellingham. It wasn't even close. I was twenty-one years old and figured I could turn things around a bit, go straight for a while, but it was a quick stint. Gang activity there was just as prevalent as it was back home. Everyone at Job Corps was from the streets like me, hustling, moving, trying to stay afloat in a world that had no intention of keeping our heads above water. It was four months of welding. Gas and flames on melting metal. Sweating in masks, staring at sparks through a small screen. But it was four months of hoopin', too. I went hard in the paint, just like the dudes back home on the street courts.

I was a late bloomer, going up a shoe size and finding my athleticism after high school. I was good, killed it at a tournament at Chadron State College. I ran circles around the other welders and anyone else who wanted to play. College scouts were looking at me.

Then, I got kicked out of Job Corps after only four months. It happened on my twenty-first birthday. Some girls came to pick me up. We drove to the liquor store, got some alcohol, and had a little party. When they dropped me back on campus, I saw the security guard sitting on a pile of bricks at a construction site. I took off running. It wasn't long before he showed up in my dorm room, where I pretended to be asleep. He knew it was me. No one else in Job Corps could run as fast.

Back to the streets.

When Job Corps didn't pan out, I enlisted in the Marines, a last-ditch effort to get on the straight and narrow. The homies threw me a party after I took the ASVAB (the Armed Services Vocational Aptitude Battery), and the recruiter told me my score was high enough to get in. The physical at MEPS (Military Entrance Processing Station) was a cakewalk. Hoopin' kept me in shape. I was in like Flynn. I stayed the night in a hotel with the other recruits after MEPS and was set to ship out at the crack of dawn. I called my dad from the lobby that night.

"Everything go all right?" Dad asked.

"Yes, sir. Everything went great." I was giddy, shaking a bit, but I held it in.

"I'm glad to hear it. Remember to keep your nose clean while you're there. Boot camp's a bitch, but it'll be over in no time."

"Yes, sir. I will." I grinned because I could hear his grin through the phone.

"And make sure to write your mother when they let you."

"I will, Dad. Tell Momma I love her. And Dad …"

"Yes, son?"

"Thank you."

"Don't thank me. You did this."

I hung up, swelling from my father's pride. One of very few times in my life when I knew I'd done right by him.

I didn't sleep. I couldn't. I'd miss the homies but not the hustle.

We were shuttled onto a bus the following morning. The driver was stocky and had a toothpick dangling from his lip. He reminded me of that cab driver from a lifetime ago, but if he was sorry, it was because his rig was loaded with half-cocked, rowdy boys who didn't know what they were getting into, a cacophony of hoots and hollers of freedom. I think the jug of coffee in his cupholder was meant to stave off the headache we most certainly caused.

We pulled out of the parking lot and were on our way to the airport, where we would fly to the Marine Corps Recruit Depot in San Diego. Halfway there, the driver turned us back around. He took us right back to the MEPS station. He turned around in his seat, shouted my name, and told me to get off the bus.

The hollers fell silent.

"What do you mean?" I asked without moving.

All eyes were on me.

"I mean I've been told to bring you back," the driver said. "We're back, so if you'd please." He pulled a lever and opened the doors.

"But I'm supposed to—"

"Look, kid, I've got a schedule to keep. I have no more information than you do, but I bet if you walk into that building, you'll find out what's going on. And I can be on my way."

I got off the bus. I watched it drive off without me, all those faces in all those windows. I had a feeling I'd never see them again, that I'd never experience the life they were off to.

A nurse met me with a somber look as I entered the building. She took me to a room and told me to wait. And when the doctor came in—the very one who had given me my physical and anointed me a perfect candidate for the Corps just one day prior —I knew something was amiss.

"Sorry about the mix-up," he said as he flipped through the documents in his hands. He didn't even look up at first, meet me eye to eye.

"What's going on?"

"Your blood work came in. I have bad news." He looked up then and must have seen the shock on my face. "You're not going to die—at least not today. But you'll need to get a primary physician and start seeing him regularly. And you won't be serving in the Marines."

"What do you mean? You said I was good to go." I had a million questions. He had but one answer.

"Well, it turns out that you're displaying traits of sickle cell anemia."

I'd find out later that sickle cell anemia is inherited, a gift from the family I never knew. It can cause fatigue, shortness of breath, dizziness, and sometimes severe pain in the joints and chest. And in the United States, ninety percent of the people who have it are Black.

I fought the tears I knew would come, at least until I was alone.

"Sorry about this, kid." I'd heard that line before, and I was damn tired of it.

I was a United States Marine for a single day. A twenty-four-hour soldier. And then I was done. Kaput. I didn't know how I'd face the homies who'd sent me off with a bang, let alone the father who'd finally approved of where I was headed. I had no prospects, no skills other than those I'd acquired on the streets, and all I could ask myself was, *what the fuck am I supposed to do?*

They say when it rains, it pours. Well, my world was a deluge of discontentment.

Then I found out my girl was pregnant.

MY GIRLFRIEND'S dad was in a motorcycle gang. When we got pregnant, he rode his Harley from Arkansas to Nebraska. He pulled up on me and said, "Make sure you take care of my daughter. Don't make me have to come back up here again." Message received. That was the only time I ever saw him.

Now, her momma was another story. Miss Taylor was also from Arkansas. She went to the same high school as Bill Clinton and brags about that all the time. Miss Taylor is one bad, streetwise woman who was not to be messed with, and she didn't care much for me. News of this pregnancy wouldn't help my cause.

Miss Taylor probably weighs all of ninety pounds, but I don't recommend underestimating this little lady. She's the snappiest dresser and has the greatest hat, shoe, and purse collection I have ever seen. She's also a professional gambler. She plays Tunk and Spades; they know her by name at the casino. After she warmed up to me, I was short on cash, and she took my $100 and tripled it.

The first time I went to the house, Miss Taylor gave me the stink eye and a tongue lashing that started with, "What the fuck you doing over here?" Looking back, I think she was testing me to see if I would stick around.

While she was cussing me out, I noticed a huge guy with a Jheri curl sprawled on the couch with his feet hanging off the end. Amigo. He just lay there like I wasn't worth his time. Turns out things like keeping a job or being faithful to Miss Taylor weren't worth his time either. He did seem to have time for drugs and another girlfriend across town. He would be at Miss Taylor's house for a while, then leave and go smoke crack with this other chick. He'd come back and argue with Miss Taylor.

When Miss Taylor had enough, she went out and bought a .45 special.

I get a call to come to the house. Amigo is planning to stop by and pick up his stuff. I take my buddy, and we head out. Amigo comes to the door, and Miss Taylor goes upstairs. When she comes back to the landing, I see the gun in her hand.

Amigo has his hands full, and he's walking toward the door. I move in behind him so she won't shoot. She follows us outside, and at the end of the block, we see his girlfriend sitting in her car.

Miss Taylor cocks the pistol and shoots. It's the middle of the day. People are outside, and the shot from the .45 is ringing in my ears. I turn to see Miss Taylor cock the gun again. The gun is an automatic, and now she's jammed it with two bullets in the chamber. Amigo makes his escape, and I take the gun from her. Later, she pays me and my buddy to shoot up the other girl-friend's house.

Miss Taylor always knew what was up. She knew I was on the streets. She was tough on me but let me stay at their house when I needed a place to stay. When I needed food, she would feed me. If I needed to wash my clothes or take a shower, she was available. Even though she gave me grief, and it was rough at times, I love her to death. To this day, I visit her in Omaha when I can. I enjoy those conversations. She's met my family. Miss Taylor is a very important part of this whole puzzle because she gave me some tough love. She was there for me when not many people were.

MY SON WAS BORN BACK in the hood. My girl handled the first months of his life like she'd handled every other day, with no other option. Valentine's Day came shortly after, and I wanted to take her out, thank her for all she'd done, so I showed up at her crib with some flowers. Her sister answered when I knocked.

"She ain't here."

"Where is she?"

"She's out, while I'm watching your kid."

"What do you mean she's out?"

"I mean she's out," she said, cold, indifferent. "She's with your boy."

"My best friend?"

"That would be him. They took the bus."

"It's like that?" I asked.

"I guess so." She raised her eyebrows and shook her head. "Nobody can tell that girl nothing."

I walked away.

"Good luck," she said. "And don't mind me. I'll just be looking after this baby."

I didn't hear her or care in the slightest about what she said. My rage burned.

I drove straight to the bus stop to wait. When they didn't show, I went back to her place and attempted to kick in the door. I called my best friend's mother, told her he had it coming. And he caught that whoopin', too. Then I called my parents. They lived in Kalamazoo, Michigan, at the time. I asked if I could stay with them for a while. I broke the phone when they said no. I told myself, *fuck it, let's get this money and do it alone*.

But we're never alone. Not truly ...

———

BETWEEN ALL THE drugs and robbery, I never stopped going to the library, devouring books on African history. In my readings, specifically in *National Geographic*, I came across Islam, the Quran, the teachings of Muhammad, and I was taken by it. Maybe it was because the religion portrayed such a stark difference from the life I was leading and desperately wished to change. Maybe I'd wished to submit to the will of Allah, something greater than myself. I remembered my first mother teaching me to pray so long before, and it had always stuck with me.

I spent a lot of time in the Old Market downtown, a great place for slingin' weed as tourists came from all over, looking for a good time. It was quick money for food, anyway. A Mellow Yellow and some Flamin' Hot Cheetos. And each time I went, I'd run into a man—Dr. Saidi J. Liwaru, big, bald, nappy beard—who spent his days selling perfume oils and incense. He took pity upon me but never judged me, and by some divine intervention or just the kindness of his heart, he reached out a hand to pull me from the darkness in which I lived.

"You know," he began, "I see you here often." A crowd of tourists bustled by. One of whom had just purchased a dub sack from me.

"Yeah," I replied with hesitance. "I'm here from time to time." I was on the corner near his stand, waiting for more customers.

"I could use your help. And I think you could use mine."

"I'm straight, old man. But thanks for the offer."

"I could pay you a little."

"No, thanks, man. I got plenty of money."

I went back to the library. I wanted to know more. I wanted to learn Arabic. I want to know Muhammad, and through him, Allah.

So, one day, after I learned how to make *wudu* and mustered the courage to do it publicly, I went to the mosque on 72nd Street. I joined a crowd so different from the ones I'd seen downtown. The men wore thobes and kufis. But the countenance of all, men and women, was deep and meditative. Their reasons for being there of the utmost importance. I wore Dickies and a t-shirt, and nothing on my head. Given the clash in language and culture, I didn't understand most of what was said or done, but for some reason, I felt I belonged.

I followed the other men to the sinks.

I knew from my readings that to perform *salah,* I must first make my intention clear in my heart and mind. And to say Bismillah—the name of Allah—before I began washing. When I reached the sink, I started with my right hand as the other men did. I rinsed it three times from fingertips to wrist before switching to my left. Then to my mouth, three rinses for it as well. I coughed a little when I took too much water on the first of three snorts. After rinsing my nose, I washed my face three times from ear to ear, just like the other men. On to my arms, the right first, three times from fingertips to elbow, then to the left. Next, I ran my wet hands from my forehead to the back of my head and then from the back of my head to my forehead. This step was done once, as was the next, which was to clean my ears. Next, the men around me stuck their feet into the sinks to wash them three times each, starting with the right. I took off my socks and followed along. Finally, we recited the Shahada and the Dua:

"Ash-hadu an la ilaha illal lahu wa ash-hadu anna Muhammadan 'abduhu wa rasuluh."

"I testify that there is no god but Allah, and I also testify that Muhammad is His servant and messenger."

"Allahuma j'alnee mina tawabeen waj-'alnee minal mutatahireen."

"O Allah, make me among those who seek repentance and make me among those who purify themselves."

Afterward, a familiar face approached.

"Assalamu alaikum," said Dr. Saidi, who stood beside another man. "Peace be upon you, brother."

"Wa alaikum salaam." I learned that from my readings as well, but I think I butchered the pronunciation on that first go. My first family had given me another gift along with the sickle cell. I am autodidactic, which means I can learn independently. I've always been able to see things like drawing, or barbering, or the tenets of Islam and quickly understand them and replicate them.

"Welcome, brother," Dr. Saidi said, hugging me tightly. "I'm so glad to see you here. This," he wrapped an arm around the other man's shoulders, "is my son."

I greeted him as well.

"I'm glad to be here," I said, and I was.

"And now, you must come with me to another mosque. On 33rd Street."

I found refuge at that second mosque. Food and shelter. A different kind of family. I stayed in the basement there for months before getting my own place. I came and went as I pleased. I took part in all prayers and eventually became responsible for the call to prayer. It was an honor. That man and that mosque helped me to understand the foundation of my beliefs. Dr. Saidi gave me a Muslim name: Sunni Alief Muhammad. He gave me work, too. And he introduced me to others who gave me work.

If only it were enough. But survival is expensive. I was still caught in the firm grasp of life on the streets. Like the tungsten fist of my father, ostensibly unbreakable, that grasp would not release until I fell much further.

MY NEW GIRL WAS A BEAUTIFUL, chocolatey gumdrop who lived in South Omaha—a completely different world from North Omaha. I spent lots of time on her side of town, which was a risk in itself.

My girl had a cousin who stopped by the crib daily, a crackhead and a prostitute, always looking to score. One day, she paid for her weed with some information about an easy target.

When the cousin showed up, my girl was braiding my hair on the front porch, braids that would have been cut had the military taken me in.

"What's up, Limpy?" She and everyone else dubbed me Limpy after a botched robbery. Someone pulled me away as I was kicking a guy, and I hyperextended my leg. I used a cane for some time after.

"What do you know, girl?"

"There's a trick," she said as I handed her the joint I was smoking. She took a long, deep hit and blew out smoke as she said, "He's got all his money. Flashing that shit."

She had my attention.

"You should come rob him, Limpy. He ain't shit."

My girl agreed: "Shit, easy money. Go grab that dough, Limpy."

So, I followed the prostitute back to the dude's apartment. She took me in, said I was her friend, and I asked to borrow his phone. He obliged, so I took the time to look around a bit.

His place wasn't much better than mine. Cracks in the walls, holes in the carpet, linoleum missing. The walls were yellow from smoke. But he had gold chains on the counter and a bundle of cash. He was too proud. I had to take him down a notch.

I put his phone down and dipped out. I had to be smart about this.

I returned a little later and told the dude I left my wallet. He let me in, sat back down, and that's when I got him. One punch. Knocked him out cold. I went through his pockets, grabbed the chains and cash, and dipped out again. Quick and clean.

When I got back to the crib, I had my girl remove my braids. I figured it was a good idea to change my appearance, just in case. And just when she'd finished, a cop car rolled up. Her cousin was in the back seat.

"Can you step down from the porch for a moment."

"I can do that," I said, innocent as could be. "What's the problem, officers?"

"We're investigating an assault. Do you mind if we take your picture?"

What choice did I have?

They snapped a Polaroid, got back in the cruiser, and drove away.

WHEN THE DUDE I robbed woke up and identified me from that Polaroid, I was done for. I just didn't know it yet. I found myself removed from the jungle and placed behind the bars of the zoo. And when it happened, like the moments before the great clock stops ticking, a whole life flashed through my mind. I saw the blurred face of my first mother, shaking from side to side; Miss Bailey and my old friend Biddy, tears and disappointment; the scowl of those who adopted me, his eyes bloodshot and drunk, hers wincing in pain; Dr. Saidi, who'd tried.

A detective came to see me within a few days in holding. He called me by my old name, but Sunni is the one I took with me to jail, what everyone else called me. He walked me in my cuffs to a cold room lit by a flickering fluorescent bulb, a little camera set up in the corner, red light on. I'd been in that room before—that room where it's just you and your choices. Everybody's gangster until they get in that room. I've seen it many times. That room and what comes after changes you. The bravado falls away. Guys who owned the streets are all about thug life until they're by themselves, crying in a corner in prison. You find out who you are in that room.

The detective wanted to know about the robbery, if I knew anything about it, or if I had anything to do with it. I was willing to own my own shit, but I wasn't going to make it easy on them. And I was never going to snitch on anybody else.

The judge asked me what I would do to a man who robbed my home—I couldn't dispute him when the gavel fell.

I was on my way to Douglas County Jail to await my sentencing date.

My girl was there. I got to see her tears fall in person. She put money on my books right away and visited as soon as they let her. It broke my heart to break hers, but I already knew it couldn't work. I'd drive myself crazy thinking about her on the outside. I gave her the title to my car, told her to think of me when she had the system bumpin'.

AT DOUGLAS COUNTY, I was placed in general population. Pods of fifty men. And they all knew who the new guy was. Barks and taunts, hollers and catcalls—the sounds of the zoo. I knew I'd have to make an impression, lest someone try to pull my card. I took a few days to get my bearings first. Shit food and milk that made me shit. Shit-brown jumpsuits. What can I say, the place was shitty.

I'd set out to prove myself and earned some time in the hole. I was happy for the respite, found solace in the seclusion.

After my first stint in the hole, I was placed in a new pod. The guards tried their best to mitigate further violence by separating those who quarreled, though some of them liked it, watched with greedy grins for a while before stepping in, like bettors at a cock-fighting ring. I recognized some of the dudes at the new pod. I'd seen them on the block.

A grapevine developed—which tends to happen when we all know the color of each other's shit—and through it, I learned that we had more inmates headed to our pod. I guess some people found out where they were going ahead of time. One of the newbies was a former associate of mine—a former associate who ratted out my brother and got him locked up at the Lincoln Correctional Center, where they sent young gang bangers. I knew what I had to do. Nobody would call me disloyal.

I waited for the day with patience. I went through the motions. Rec time, chow times, lights out. Other than the whole not being able to leave, I suppose life wasn't all that different than if I were in the military. Not yet anyway. And when the day did come, I gathered my things—snacks, extra shower shoes—and gave it all away. I knew I wouldn't be back. I was headed to my place of respite, a little vacation. I sat on the edge of my bed, that scratchy blanket on a thin pad, and waited for the doors to the pod to pop open, for the snitch to walk through them.

He had his own scratchy blanket in his arms, along with a stained pillow, a magazine, and some hygiene items. Looking back, I see how scared he was, sweating, trembling, shifty. But at the time, I didn't care. I beelined straight to him.

"What up?" I saw immediate recognition. He knew me.

"Hey, ma—"

I didn't wait. Fuck him.

I got my second Code Blue—a handy little system that alerted the tax-paid sentries to our position—after just a couple of weeks in that new pod.

Word of me was flourishing.

AFTER MY SECOND stint in the hole, I was placed in a unit, two stories of two-man cells. That vacation lasted for about a month. No more pods for me. It was like they were rewarding me. I could take a shit in peace!

The dudes in that unit liked to play cards …

"I heard you've been reckless in here," an old head from Chicago said as he shuffled the deck. He wore glasses. Had some gray in his beard. Lines in his face that a man can only get from the streets. I'd soon learn that he had gang ties dating back to the sixties with some violent motherfuckers.

"Nah," I said as I shrugged my shoulders. "I'm just doing my thing."

"Heard you were part of the club, too," he said.

"You hear a lot of things."

He stopped shuffling. Looked me dead in the eyes.

I pulled my collar, showed him the brand on my chest.

"How'd you get blessed in?" Back to shuffling. The dudes around him looked up. The question was a test.

"I wasn't," I said straight up. "Not officially. I just met some dudes on the courts back home. They raised me up, taught me the signs, the lit, and put me to work." I shrugged again. "And now I'm here."

One of the other dudes sucked his teeth and shook his head. Like I wasn't real.

I found myself balling my fist, puffing my chest. I stayed ready. My card was stowed securely.

But the man who had shuffled the cards put a hand on the dude, "It's all good," he said. "It's all good. Boy's proven himself. More than some of you." And then back to me, "Come sit down and play."

And from that moment on, I looked after that old man. Played chess and spades with him. I learned he was human—more than an OG. Affiliated with the tip top. He had clout, and with it, he gave me my official stamp. I was in now, with connections across the jungle and zoos, even the big one. I kept the name Sunni.

My third Code Blue came when a skinhead entered our unit. He went right to his cell amid the glares of Black men, and he knew better than to come back out.

"He's got to go," the big man said. And his word was all I needed.

I saved my milk. Let it spoil. Let it stink. It didn't take long to coagulate. Then I waltzed over to the skinhead's cell and tossed it in.

"What the fuck?" He stood, swiping at the slightly yellow curdles splattered across his torso. The stench was unreal.

It took one hit when he crossed the threshold out of his cell. I felt a bone crack beneath my white knuckles. He went to sleep.

I went on vacation for another month.

———

I WENT BACK to my unit after that stint and wouldn't be back for that peace and quiet until after I had a tooth removed, and that time, I requested the hole. Luckily, the guard on duty was cool. My mouth was gushing. The doctor said I had to go on a soup diet. I would lose some weight in the process. I couldn't go back to the unit looking like a bitch.

I WAS in county for eight months by the time sentencing day came. That detective said he'd see me again and see he did as he watched me take my seat in shackles. I got the same judge, and he was quick and stern. It felt like less than five minutes that time.

Three

To

Six

Years

for the only offense I'd ever been caught up for.

The gavel dropped.

I was in the news.

And I was headed to Nebraska State Penitentiary. The big zoo.

Back at the Douglas County Jail, I sat down just in time for the latest episode of *The Fresh Prince of Bel-Air*, knowing it would take my mind off things. Carlton's dumbass dances and Will's loudass laughs always got me going. The others watching were laughing, too, when this dude we called Oklahoma waltzed in.

"I want to watch the news," Oklahoma said. Before anyone had a chance to respond, he stepped right in front of us and turned the channel.

The other boys did nothing.

I kept my cool. How could he know what kind of day I had? So, I went over and flipped the channel back. "Nah," I said, "that shit will be on again later. We're watching *Fresh Prince*." I took my seat.

"I'm watching the news," said this brave man. He flipped the damn channel again.

When I went to change it back, Oklahoma swatted my hand away like I was a child, reaching into the cookie jar without permission.

I shoved him back. He lunged forward and bit me on the chest. Then it was off, and not for the pain. I didn't feel pain when triggered, I just didn't want his dirty ass mouth on me.

My next Code Blue was for beating the brakes off that dude. Guards ripped us apart, three to each of us like we were King Kong and Godzilla, and they put us on the ground before I did too much damage.

"Fuck you," said Oklahoma, spitting blood, struggling with the three bodies that weighed him down.

"Shut your fucking mouth, inmate," said one of the guards, knee on Oklahoma's back.

I smiled at Oklahoma, who never fucked with me again. Other than the zigzag of his crooked teeth on my chest, I didn't have a mark on me.

**MY INMATE ID FROM
THE NEBRASKA DEPARTMENT
OF CORRECTIONS.**

I was determined that prison
wouldn't define my identity.

THEY SHACKLED me and put me on a bus headed west to Lincoln. I stared out the window, Snoop Dogg's "Murder Was the Case" running through my mind. I arrived first at the Nebraska Diagnostic and Evaluation Center, a maximum custody reception center where they sort the animals, classify us, grade our threat level, tell us which programs we'll have to take part in, and then send us on our way. The whole process takes about ninety days.

I learned the rules right away at D & E:

1. Don't gamble. You get got for debts.
2. Don't borrow shit. You get got for debts.
3. Don't do drugs. You get got for debts, and more time for getting high.
4. Mind your business and keep your mouth shut. Some people get got just for seeing shit.
5. Don't rep your gang or hood. It tallies up when one group takes life from another. And like I said, you get got for debts.

EASY ENOUGH, ostensibly. But trouble's always lingering when you're incarcerated. Fuck else is there to do?

ON MY FIRST day at the Nebraska State Penitentiary, I went to the library. They couldn't stop me from reading, and then, more than ever before, I wanted to lean into my heritage and Islam. I would fill my brain with African culture and the words of Muhammad.

The first thing I saw when I got to the stacks: Two men fucking.

Welcome to prison.

THE BIG MAN I'd met at Douglas County had a gift waiting for me when I got to my cell that first day in the big zoo. A box of goodies. Magazines, food, deodorant, everything of comfort us animals were allowed to possess. The other associates let me know it was him and that I had people on the inside. My new job was to protect this young cat from Chicago who was in for drug trafficking. He also had a gambling problem, and that gambling problem put him in debt to a formidable "family." The young cat broke Rule 1 before he even showed up.

Sometimes gifts come with strings attached.

One of the boys from the "family" was a big man. He looked like Tommy "Tiny" Lister Jr., Deebo from *Friday*. He was sinister, too. Menacing. Once, over a game of chess, he described to me in detail how to dispose of a body with a straight face and a matter-of-fact tone. He didn't smile. He didn't chuckle to make me think he was joking. He didn't even whisper to hide the fact that he was a killer. Though I didn't show it, I got chills thinking about how many bodies it took him to perfect his craft. I wasn't exactly inclined to put his king in check, either; everyone knew not to get on his bad side. Even after all the talk of murder, he was known for one thing on the inside: he liked to rape other dudes.

So, one day, I was lying in my bunk, hands interlaced beneath my head, feet crossed and kicked up. I was daydreaming about what I'd do when I got out when a dude ran into my cell to tell me that this monster was choking out the young cat. I was dazed at first, not ready to let go of the daydream, but eventually, I tilted my head over to see through the community room and into the hall-way. He had the young cat up against the wall between two phones.

I jumped up. Time to go to work.

"This motherfucker owes me," the monster said as I walked into the hallway. The young cat struggled to breathe but wasn't putting up much of a fight.

"Let him go, man." I didn't want to fight—didn't want a rift between his family and my associates—but I was ready with two balled fists at my waist.

"Fuck that. It's time he pays up." The monster looked at me again, this time with a wide grin. "Why don't you turn around and guard the hall for me." He nodded past me to the community room. "I'm about to make this young cat my little bitch." The young cat showed a surge of struggle then, but it was futile beneath the weight of the monster's massive arm.

I swung, not with all my might, but with enough force to show the monster I wasn't about to let the homie get fucked in the ass.

He released the young cat, who choked and stumbled further down the hall with his hands on his neck.

"It's like that?" the monster asked. He squared up to me.

"It's like that," I said with a shrug. My balled fists were in front of my face. *Fuck it.*

Then he walked right past me with another grin, and I knew he was about to confer with his cousins about fucking with my associates.

I immediately got suited and booted—khakis, boots, a beanie, and work gloves. I stuffed some *National Geographic* magazines beneath my clothes for extra protection around my vital areas. The monster liked to use knives.

Word spread quickly. We all knew it was going down, but I wanted to speak to my superior first. So, I stayed back when everyone went to dinner.

"I already heard about what happened," my boss said.

"I figured," I replied. "I wanted to come to you before anything went down."

My boss stood and gestured with two fingers as he said, "Let's have a little sit down."

It turns out the monster didn't go to dinner either. He sat in the community room with his cousin, who offered my boss a seat across from him. I remained standing.

"We got a problem," said the monster's cousin.

"Looks that way," my boss said. "What can we do to fix it?"

"I want mine," the monster snapped, but his cousin raised a hand to silence him.

"See, monster here has needs, and your boy didn't respect that."

I kept my mouth shut.

"I want the young cat in the showers," the monster said. "Tonight."

"That can't happen," my boss said.

"How else do you expect to set this right?"

I wasn't about to let this happen, so I said, "I'll fight him."

The monster looked up at me with that evil grin of his.

But my boss was prepared. He slid a packet across the table. "Smoke it. Sell it. But either way, let's just call this a misunderstanding and move on."

The monster's cousin picked up the packet and smiled. "Looks like you'll have to find another fish to take the showers tonight."

But the monster wasn't satisfied. He wanted blood. "You're gonna let Sunni pop me like that and just walk away?"

"There is the matter of respect, even after your generous donation."

My boss sighed. "We ain't got nothing else for you—"

"One hit," I said, looking directly at the monster. "I got you one time. Hit for hit."

"One to the chest from our enforcer," my boss said. They'd never let the monster lay hands on any of us. Our enforcer would be his proxy. The enforcer was the biggest dude in our association. He could put 315 on the bench press and workout with it, and he was fast. He could have been a star in the NFL if he hadn't been on the streets and caught for running cocaine.

"Not good enough," his cousin said. "The monster is too hungry for one hit."

"We'll give the young cat ten to the chest, too." My boss sighed.

The monster cracked his knuckles. "We can make that work."

"Go get the young cat," my boss told me.

I took my hit, and then the enforcer turned to the young cat. He went down hard. Blood pooled. We didn't see him for three days after, but everything had been put right. The young cat wasn't fucked with again.

The monster is now on death row. That's probably a gift for everybody.

LIKE ON THE STREETS, you learn to be vigilant behind bars. One gang had a leader who was as big as Suge Knight. He liked to talk. Loud talk. Shit talk. The kind of talk that got under the skin of rivals. Tension broke out on the weight pile at the end of the gym one day when he started talking, and members of another set didn't take it so well.

Word spread through the yard: it's going down at five o'clock when doors pop. We all got ready in case things spilled over—at least the smart ones did.

Our leaders told us to be in the gym on the bleachers, facing the door. Five o'clock, we were in place. The big guy's crew was at the weight pile. They did not look ready. The gym door opened, and six members of the rival gang came in single file. They walked the long way around the gym toward the pile right past us, steely resolve on their faces.

When they got to the weights, big guy started talkin'. The guy at the head of the line threw something from a Styrofoam cup into his face. The next two in line pulled knives and started stabbing the big guy. He tried to fight back with a weight, but none of his homies stepped in to help. The next two guys in line stepped up and started stabbing. It was a precision attack. We stayed on the bench watching until the alarms went off. Time to scatter.

We ran to the yard and hit the deck when the guard fired a warning shot from the tower. I looked up from the dirt and saw the big guy stagger out of the gym. He made it a few steps before collapsing in a pool of blood.

Somehow, he survived. Must have been all the layers between the blades and his internal organs.

———

MY FIRST PAROLE hearing was a joke. I think they just wanted to see my reaction to their denial. I didn't even go to the second one. Fuck 'em, I thought. But at my third hearing, after all that I'd gone through, the members of the board deemed me remediated. And I kept that shit to myself. The big man from Douglas County and my boss at the pen were the only two people who knew I was getting out.

I'd watched and learned. When you get ready to leave the pen, you can't tell anybody on the inside because you never know how they'll react. One inmate made the mistake of telling the guy he was dating that he was getting out and going home to his wife. One area of the yard near the tennis courts and slightly off the guards' radar was where inmates would bury shanks in the dirt. The boyfriend went to the tennis court and grabbed a shank. When he saw his lover, he started stabbing. The guy put up his hands to protect his face, clueless that he should have kept his good news to himself.

AFTER TWO YEARS in the Nebraska State Penitentiary, I went to the Nebraska Correctional Treatment Center for six months where I worked as a secretary alongside some of the sweetest White women I'd ever met. Never once did those old birds treat me like a convicted felon, just a dude who had no clue what the hell he was doing.

"What do you mean, 'search bar,'" I asked. I was looking for a job I could do when I was processed out, and although I'd heard of the internet, I'd never seen it up close.

"Right here." Myrna tapped her painted fingernail on the glass screen of the computer in front of me. She was petite, patient, walked with a hunch, and had cheeks that hung below her jaw. "Type: Jobs in Lincoln, Nebraska."

I jabbed at the keys with two index fingers. A long list of links appeared. "Look at you," I said, "keeping up with all the fancy new tech."

Myrna chuckled, "I'm not dead yet."

"No, ma'am. And neither am I."

"Now you're off." Myrna turned to hobble away. "Good luck."

I spent the rest of my shift browsing for jobs, filling out online applications, checking sports standings, reading the news. I was in awe of all that I had missed. They also had *Encyclopedia Britannica* on disc. I spent hours falling down one rabbit hole after another.

DISCOVERY

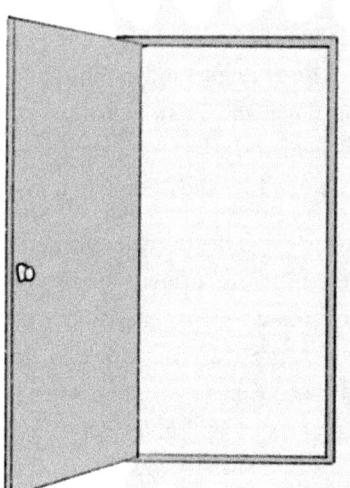

IT WAS 1999. I was twenty-five years old and on work release. In prison, I'd done a reset and altered the way I presented myself in the world. I changed the way I talked, code-switching to create a different image. I lost weight and intentionally stopped lifting so I didn't appear huge and intimidating. I researched what I needed to look polished and what it meant to be a gentleman—so many layers. This helped me land a job when I got out.

I got a job in downtown Lincoln at a telemarking company. I'd had some experience before prison—about two weeks. I was fired from the job because I kept missing work. I'd get pulled over by the police on my way to work and not make it to my job. After a month with a headset and a long list of numbers, I was promoted to team lead and given an office and a desk with my name on it. I had learned how to talk to people on the streets, how to sell, how to persuade, and how not to take any bullshit. So, talking to people over the phone came easy enough. Make it fun was my mantra, and my team followed suit. Everybody wanted to be on my team. Our sales numbers were solid.

One day, I started getting notes on my desk.

Have a nice day!

Hope your day goes well!

Stuff like that. At first, I didn't know who they were from, but I figured out it was one of two girls on my team. I was freaking out because these girls were digging me, but I didn't want to mess it up and say, "Hey, thanks for the notes," to the wrong person! I was in suspense but eventually learned who it was. We started kind of talking. We went out on a date, got some food—super simple. We went to the house where I was paroled and sat on the couch playing video games. One thing led to another, and we had sex.

We got pregnant that night. First try. My mind flashed back to the woman I'd loved in Bellingham, Washington. When we got pregnant, she'd had an abortion. It boggled my mind. Abortion wasn't an option in my book. So, I was ecstatic when my girlfriend, who later became my wife, got pregnant. I wasn't at all afraid. This time, I was going to be a real father.

We kept our relationship—and the pregnancy—quiet for as long as we could. I was not supposed to be dating someone from my job. I was her boss, and I was breaking the rules. When she started showing, she wore baggy clothes.

When my girlfriend told me she was pregnant, I thought, "Shit, I'm going to be a dad. I've got to get a better job!" I also needed something better to drive than a beat-up, raggedy old car I'd paid four hundred dollars for—a Pontiac 3000 with no air-conditioning or heat. I couldn't imagine strapping a car seat into the back seat.

I remembered someone had told me I should think about selling cars. "Car salesmen make a bunch of money, man." I knew I was a good salesman. I already had a second job, working part-time at Ben Simon's, a men's clothing store. It carried nice men's clothes for climbers like me, and I worked there to buy my clothes—

stylin' suits. I wore one when I drove to the Anderson used car lot on my lunch break from the telemarketing job and asked them for a job.

"Have you ever sold cars before?"

"Nope."

Like most jobs I've had since prison, I had to go before some board and explain my mistakes, tell them what happened, ask for a chance, and say, "See me now." For this job, I had to go before both the state parole board and the board that would license me to sell cars. They cleared me, and I got the job at Anderson Ford. Let me tell you, I was motivated! The dealership had what they called a demo program. If a salesman sold twenty cars in three months, they would receive a demo car to drive around; a mutually beneficial arrangement that would promote the business and let the salesman roll in style. I made it my goal. I had a baby coming, and I did not want to pick them up from the hospital in this freakin' hooptie. It was hot outside. I mean hot! I'd wear a shirt and tie to work, and by the time I drove to work in that rust bucket with no A/C, I was drenched. It was ridiculous.

I told the manager, "I have a baby on the way, and I want a demo."

"Well, sell twenty cars, and you can get a demo," he said. At that time, they only had a couple of guys who were selling that many cars. But as I said, I was motivated. I ended up selling twenty cars in the first month! They gave me a demo the second month. They didn't even wait the full amount of time. I'll never forget the black Mazda 5—nothing fancy. It was a base model, but for me, it was brand new, and it even had a bumpin' sound system. It meant I could pick up my daughter and her mama in a sweet ride!

Early on, my girlfriend and I started playing a game. I don't know why. She always wanted to race me to the car, race me to the house. It was her deal. She continued it even when she was pregnant. She would waddle along, and it was hilarious. I never tried to beat her. One day, she sprinted out, had on the wrong shoes, and just tackled the stairs to the house. When I saw how banged up she was, I panicked. I picked her up and raced to the car, running every red light to zoom her to the hospital so they could check her and make sure she and the baby were okay. They were both fine at that time, but my baby girl did come about a month and a half early. It probably had nothing to do with that fall.

The night our daughter was born, her mom and I had gone to see *Eyes Wide Shut*, a steamy film with Tom Cruise. When we got home, we were thinking about doing some adult things when, suddenly, her water broke. I felt the bed was wet and asked, "Did you just pee?" We were like rookies; we didn't know anything.

"Oh my God, my water broke!" She said.

We didn't know what to do. We called an Ask a Nurse helpline, and they told us to get to the hospital. Of course, there's no turning back once the water breaks, so they induced labor. I fell asleep sitting next to her. It was a long labor. I'd wake up when they came in to check her, and when I heard, "She's only at six centimeters," I'd fall back asleep. I wasn't awake when the baby's head started showing. I woke up more when all chaos was ensuing. The room was filled with doctors, nurses and machines. They were saying, "All right, it's time to push." My girlfriend pushed once or twice, and our baby girl popped out!

"Oh, my god, this baby's here!"

I was in a fog. They asked me if I wanted to cut the umbilical cord, and even though I was barely awake, I said, "Yes." It's almost a blur.

Here's this tiny baby girl—four pounds, four ounces. She was so little that they put the IV in her head. She was in an incubator for a while before she came home. But it was funny—she went from being a preemie to being the fattest baby ever. Dillard's Department store used to have a Cutest Baby contest, and my daughter won it! We got gift cards and bought baby clothes, and they put her picture up in the store. I was so proud.

Watching my girlfriend (later to be my wife) hold that baby made me feel—real. It gave me a new purpose. One of my fears was always passing on the generational curse. I wanted to be a curse breaker. I did not want my kids to go through what I went through, so I set out to raise them, parent them differently, break the cycle, and help them be more successful than I was. Our baby girl's birth was the beginning.

MY FAMILY TREE BEGINS WITH ME.

TOP: Helping my son with homework.
BOTTOM: My wife and four of my children.

EMERGENCE

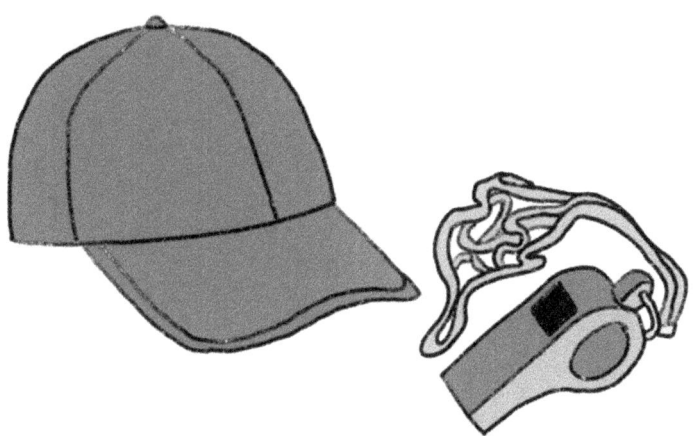

BUZZ. *Buzz. Buzz.*

The busy single echoed through the landline all the way from Virginia to my home in Lincoln, Nebraska.

Then that voice.

"All circuits are busy. Please try your call again later."

I'd heard that damn lady's voice a hundred times by then. Still, I tried again.

It was my day off from the car dealership. My daughter's mother called me just after nine that morning and told me to turn on the TV. And you know what I saw. Everybody saw it. A plane flying directly into the south tower of the World Trade Center while the north tower billowed black smoke. A plane had hit that tower seventeen minutes earlier. I watched. Stunned. Just like everybody else. Then they started talking about a plane hitting the Pentagon, and I freaked out.

Buzz. Buzz. Buzz.

Buzz. Buzz. Buzz.

"All circuits are busy. Please try your call again later."

My adoptive father worked at the Pentagon.

Buzz. Buzz. Buzz.

Two days later, I finally reached my parents, who were living in Woodbridge, Virginia. On September 11, 2001, my adoptive dad was on a break from his job inside the Pentagon. He was sitting outside on a park bench and watched American Airlines Flight 77 hit the E Ring of the five-sided building. He got lucky. I got shook.

I started thinking about my parents, especially my mom. She had been sick, and I wanted to help and support her. My dad was working long hours and couldn't be home to take care of her as she needed. So, we agreed that I would move to Virginia and help out. In early 2002, I left my baby daughter and her mother in Lincoln and headed east.

Just five months after the 9/11 attacks, I drove into Washington, DC. Rocket launchers were strategically placed around the city. What the hell? It reminded me of military bases. I'd never seen heavy artillery in civilian areas.

I got a job selling cars. Now, I had been very successful selling cars in Nebraska, but this was a different game. You'll find auto dealerships all along Jefferson Davis Highway from Fredericksburg to Alexandria. I worked for one of the big ones, Lustine Toyota. On Saturday mornings, sales guys would line up in front of the dealership. The last thing you wanted was for people to drive to the next block and go to some other dealership. So, there'd be twenty dudes standing out in front. When a car pulled into the lot, the first person to step off the curb got that customer. That raises the competition, and many of these guys were really aggressive. I was following the rules and stepping off the curb when another guy sprinted over to the customers. I didn't say anything to him then, but I caught him in the hallway later and told him if he ever stepped in front of me like that again, we were gonna have to fight. That's how much of a shark tank selling cars in Virginia was. I had worked with one couple for more than four hours on a deal only to have them walk out because of the high pressure applied in the finance office. When they walked out, the sales manager followed them, screaming, then threw the folder with all the paperwork at them in the parking lot. They were definitely never coming back.

I hadn't been in the DC area even a year when terror struck again. My parents had moved from Woodbridge, about fifty minutes south to Fredericksburg. I was renting a house with five other guys. In September, we heard news about random shootings in Maryland—a restaurant owner and a liquor store employee. We didn't think much of it. Shootings happened all the time in the metro area. Then, on October 2, 2002, shit got real.

A bullet whizzed through the window at a Michael's craft store in Aspen Hill. An hour later, a man was gunned down at a grocery store. The next morning, four people were killed. One was mowing his lawn; one was pumping gas. A woman was killed sitting on a bench waiting for a bus, another while vacuuming out her car at a gas station. Panic set in.

I got off work late and had to get gas before I went home. I stopped at the gas station and watched a guy filling up. He got out of his car, ducked down, and snuck around his car to put the nozzle in the gas tank, crept back to the driver's door, got in his car, and ducked below the window. When the tank was full, he got out and zigzagged to the building to pay. I'll never forget that. People were terrified. I filled my tank as I usually did. In my mind, where I was from, how I grew up, and what I had seen already, I figured there was nothing I could do. He's a sniper, so he knows what he's doing. Your zigzagging to the building won't stop nothing.

The shootings continued over three weeks—another Michael's store, Home Depot, near a middle school, at more gas stations. I didn't get scared until the sniper shot somebody in a mall near my parents. My mom and dad were mall walkers. They would get up early and walk through the mall before the stores opened.

I was at work when I heard about the mall shooting. I dialed their home.

Buzz. Buzz. Buzz.

"All circuits are busy. Please try your call again later."

IT WAS 9/11 all over again. All I could do was watch on television. They shut down Interstate 95 and went car-to-car trying to find the shooter. I eventually got ahold of my parents, and they were fine, but I'll never forget the fear I saw in the people around me. And it made me homesick.

The entire time I was in the DC area, I'd been calling my daughter and her mother back home. I had tried dating in DC, but I didn't feel the same as when I was with the woman I'd left back in Nebraska. So, being the romantic I am, I picked up the phone and dialed the familiar number.

"Listen," I said, "You want to get married?"

CHAPTER
TWENTY-ONE
WITH CINDY

WE GOT MARRIED, and I went back to selling cars. I brought a little swagger back from my experience in DC, and I soon had a job in finance.

About a week after we got married, I got my official welcome back to the Midwest. We had a nice little bit of money from wedding gifts, and somebody gave us a gift certificate to a furniture store in a small town about twenty miles north of Lincoln. We were excited to get us some furniture.

We had a great time shopping and picking out things for our home. We were on Highway 77, driving back to Lincoln, when my wife said, "Don't look."

A green Ford Ranger pickup with a topper pulled up next to the passenger side and held a sign up in the window.

"Don't look," she said again.

The card had three letters on it: KKK. The truck pulled in front of us, and I was staring at a big Confederate flag in the back window. It was a gut punch that sucked the joy of our newlywed bliss. Someone felt like they needed to put this mixed-race couple in their place. They had to remind me who I was—or at least how they saw me.

———————

I SETTLED into a more stable life in Lincoln than I had known. I was good at my job in the auto finance industry and worked at almost every dealership in the area, following the best offers. Our family was growing. Elijah joined his older sister, Asya, in 2003. Sophia was born in 2005, and Solomon joined our family three years later.

I learned how to navigate life as a Black man in a White community. When you live in Nebraska, you are like a fly in milk. It'd be different if I were in Atlanta, Detroit, or someplace where I wasn't a minority. So, I used my smile and laugh as protection. I always twirled my keys so people could hear me coming. I lost weight and quit lifting so I would be less imposing. I went from 220 down to about 190.

And then I went back to wearing suits. For me, a suit is the ultimate coat of armor. Ask yourself this question: How many African American males have ever been shot wearing a suit? The only ones you'll ever think of are Martin Luther King Jr. and Malcolm X. I get treated differently when I wear a suit. It's like night and day how I get treated. I'm the same person in both cases, but when I wear a suit and walk into the room, they think I'm the authority figure. I'm the boss or something. People get a little more nervous if I walk into a room in a hoodie and jeans. This was the only defense I knew that was non-aggressive.

One day I had to stay late with a customer at the dealership and my brain was fried. It was a long day, and I was starving. I stopped at a neighborhood grocery store to get something to eat. When I walked into the store, I could not remember why I was there. I stood in the grocery aisle thinking, "This isn't good. This is not a healthy lifestyle." I was making good money but working seventy hours a week. I also struggled with the lack of integrity in the car business.

A global recession had led to a decline in auto sales, which meant we had to work harder than ever to sell cars. I felt bad about taking someone who was already in debt and, just because they had a desire to get a better vehicle, rolling what they owed into this new vehicle and burying them in more debt. This business model made lots of money, but people would drive off the lot and already be ten grand in the hole on their new car. It didn't sit well with me. I felt like a taker. I truly felt like all I did was take, take, take.

Something had to change. I enrolled at the community college and started taking classes. I also volunteered at the YMCA and found a new identity: Coach.

MY FIRST GIG for the Y was coaching fourth or fifth graders in basketball. I'd never coached before this, and I was never the greatest basketball player, but it was basketball season when I was looking to sign up for this deal. I coached one season of basketball and then three seasons of flag football. Even though this was a volunteer deal, I was very thorough. I was a student and still had a full-time job, but I made sure my team had a playbook. Our practices were very structured. I went out and did all the research I could to learn how to coach.

Because I'm an autodidact, I tend to learn quickly and gorge on information. If you say to me, "I wonder what it's like to build a car?" If that's something I'm interested in, I will figure out how to build a car. I will do whatever I have to do to figure out how to build it. That's how I approached coaching, and the results showed on the field.

The third season I met a couple whose son was my quarterback. They thought I'd done a great job and asked if I ever considered coaching high school football. They were teachers at Lincoln East High School and introduced me to the East High Football Coach, John Gingery. We hit it off right away. Coach Ging (rhymes with bing), as I called him, had a son who had lots of struggles in life and passed away. When Ging looked at me, he saw a guy who had had all those struggles and was trying to pull his shit together. So, he gave me a volunteer role as a reserve coach. But it came with a few hoops.

To even get into the building as a volunteer coach, I had to pass a security clearance and background checks. I had to explain why I had been in prison and detail my life since I'd been out. Once I was cleared, I started coaching wide receivers on the Spartan reserve team. I was also the Get Back Coach during Friday night games. That meant I kept our players and coaches behind the white stripes on the sidelines, even when the game was intense. I have a loud, commanding voice, so when I yelled, "GET BACK!" everyone did.

One of the men I met at Lincoln East was Coach Nelson. He was head coach for the Spartan Reserves and was also part of a group working on a new startup called Hudl, a company that is now the leader in sports video and data. Coach Nelson would invite me to their office to play with their program to see if I could break it. I loved viewing the videos and the analysis. It sparked my quest for information. I became a true student of the game of football to the point where when I was watching games on television at home, I had a notebook out in front of me, and I drew the plays they ran. I recorded games of the teams I liked or the offense I wanted to run on VHS. Then, I would go back and watch each play at least eleven times so I could see what each player did. I drew up those plays and created playbooks. Somebody caught wind of what I was doing, and I quickly became the go-to football play guy.

"You got the '86 Bear's playbook?"

"You have Clemson's playbook?"

I had all that. I was collecting everything. People would ask me for drills and all kinds of stuff.

I'd been a volunteer coach at Lincoln East for four years. I was looking for a new job and wanted to coach, but it seemed like paid coaching positions were slow to come. I took a job as a secure entrance monitor at Lincoln High School, and the head coach at High asked me to join his staff as offensive coordinator.

When I made that move in 2015, Lincoln had six public high schools. It had been four years since any Lincoln team had won the Class A football championship. Omaha area schools pretty much dominated Class A. Lincoln High had played in one championship game. It lost the 1992 crown to cross-town rival Lincoln Southeast 17-0.

Coach Macke asked me to create a playbook for his offense. During games, I was up in the booth calling plays. In my first year as the OC at Lincoln High School, we won four games—the most they'd won in eleven years. I had two great running backs, and we were the number two rushing offense in the state. We were moving in the right direction.

Lincoln has always felt inferior to the Omaha schools when it comes to football. This gap made Lincoln coaches desperate for an answer. Lincoln was home to a top-level select youth football team, the Star City Silverbacks. Coach Macke wanted to secure those players for the Lincoln High roster, so he developed a relationship with the Silverback's coach. By my second season, Macke started bringing me new play ideas. I knew they came from the Silverbacks. I was still responsible for running the offensive practices and installing our offense, but come game day, Coach would ignore the plays I called in from the booth and try something different—something our team hadn't practiced. I wish he would have talked to me, and we could have worked together to incorporate some of those ideas into the offense, but that's not how it went down.

We lost a game we should have won on some questionable play calls. When I came out of the booth, parents were lined up to yell at me and ask what the hell I was thinking. I kept my mouth shut. I walked to the parking lot, got in my car, and yelled at my wife. The guilt washed over me immediately. Shit. What was I doing? I finished the season, but my time as a coach for Lincoln High was over.

I see the potential in all student-athletes, and from day one, my philosophy has been to use football to teach life skills and to help students build memories. Everything I do as a coach stems from that. One of my favorite stories from my time at Lincoln High is about Johnny Nguyen. Johnny came from an immigrant family and had never played football in his life. He loved the game and wanted to be part of the team. Johnny was short and stocky, and when he was on the field during practice, he often got ping-ponged around. But he stuck with it. Near the end of the season, I got him in a game on special teams. Johnny made a shoe-string tackle to prevent a punt return, and he talks about it to this day.

That's why I coach—for the Johnny Nguyens. It's easy to coach the stars, but to coach players who have never played the game and come away with a memory is why I do it.

The irony is that I took over as general manager for the Silver-backs youth football program. The job sucked because of the parents. This was a select team, and every parent believed their kid should be an NFL starter one day. Youth sports are hell for coaches. In reality, only two of the kids on that team went on to play at even the college level.

Still, I wanted to build a healthy relationship between youth foot-ball and high school football in Lincoln without undermining coaches on either side. I knew it was the only way we could get close to being competitive with Omaha, which has a strong middle school football program in the public schools. I wanted our youth football coaches to get great quality coaching from the high school coaches, and I couldn't understand why they weren't connecting with the high school programs where their kids would eventually play. So, I started a clinic for youth football coaches.

I contacted all the high school head coaches, told them about this clinic, and asked if they'd be willing to come and speak. I arranged for free food from Lamar's Donuts and Chick-fil-A. Only four youth coaches showed up that first year, but I stuck with it. We've grown every year. By our fourth year, we were meeting at Hudl headquarters and had more than fifty youth coaches. One of the highlights was the Q&A panel at the end of the day, where the youth coaches could ask the high school coaches questions. After COVID, we brought coaches back together with a special clinic called Lunch with the Legend. I interviewed my old friend, Coach John Gingery, for an hour and a half while youth coaches listened in.

The clinic is now in its tenth year, and I hope it will last forever. Legacy motivates me. I like the idea that I can give these positive things to the public, and they can grow and form a life of their own. They ask me to show up for the clinics now, but I don't have to speak or do anything. I shake some hands and say thanks for coming. That's a win in my book.

IN THE SPRING OF 2016, I got a call from Greg Nelson, who was coaching at Lincoln Lutheran High School.

"How would you feel about being my wide receiver's coach?"

It was a pay cut, but I thought this might be an opportunity for me to get with a team where I could have some sway, and we could make some hay.

The previous season had been rough for Lincoln Lutheran. They finished that 2015 season 0-9 and lost six times by more than thirty points. What I did was I brought the juice and the swagger. I told the kids, "I'm the best receiver's coach in this state, and if you listen to what I say, you're going to be some of the best receivers in this state. You're going to make marks." They believed me.

I started working with the receivers before the 2016 season. I took them to the field by my house, and we started working. We went 7-2 that first year but did not make the playoffs, and I was freaking out. We go 7-2 and don't make the playoffs? What the hell we got to do?

The next year, we went 7-2 again and made the class C2 state playoffs. We won the first round 35-0 against North Platte St. Patrick's, then beat Arcadia-Loup City 21-12 on our way to the semifinals. That was the coldest game I have ever coached, and it ended when Centennial used one of our trick plays against us.

When COVID arrived in the spring of 2020, we had no idea it would disrupt fall football. By the time the season was supposed to start in August, we had teams dropping out, all kinds of scheduling problems, and we no longer had access to the stadium at Nebraska Wesleyan University, where we played our games. We moved the games back to our small home field. We had to rent lights, which created the most unique ambiance I've ever seen for a football game. When you were on the field, you couldn't see the crowd. Imagine it being dark and having just one big spotlight on the football field. That's all you saw.

Even before COVID, life was taking a toll. I was extra busy, and my sickle cell disease was flaring up. I hinted that this might be my last season, but I didn't tell anyone I was in crisis. I had been pissing blood for three weeks, but I wanted to be there for the team. I knew I needed to stop coaching for a while because of my health, so I approached that season differently. I determined to be in the moment, to focus on the details. The grass. The weather. The conversations. The kids' faces. I have an image burned in my mind from one cold evening under the portable lights. We won the game with a late score. I saw it coming. Everybody was freaking out, and I decided to be still and soak in the full scene like a panorama. The coaches were all high-fiving, and the kids were hugging. And I just stood there calmly and watched it all. I just loved it. It was amazing.

So, 2020 was my final football season as a football coach, and it left a void. After I recovered from surgery to remove my gall bladder, I almost didn't know what to do with myself. I would sit at home at night, but the ongoing disruption of COVID helped me reset and move on to new things. I now enjoy having the time to watch my youngest son play varsity football. He was named all-state honorable mention.

TOP: On the sidelines.
CENTER: Coching up one of my players.
BOTTOM: My early YMCA teams.

MY CHILDHOOD TRAUMA, educational struggles, and experience in the judicial system became tools for me when I began working at Lincoln High School. I started as a secure entry monitor before being promoted to campus supervisor. I loved interacting with kids and helping them succeed. I was often asked to check in with certain kids. Eventually, I had so many kids assigned to me that it became a miniature caseload. While I loved the work with the kids, it became overwhelming.

I was interested in advancing my career, but when I interviewed for a promotion within Lincoln Public Schools, I couldn't get any traction. They always gave me the "you had a great interview" elevator speech when they decided to go with another candidate. I was frustrated because I did not want to have to go back to school. I had my associate's degree and, at that point, wasn't interested in going to school to get another degree.

I was also in charge of the African American caucus club at Lincoln High, which consisted of forty kids. We would attend symposiums at the University of Nebraska, plan events for Black History Month, and bring in speakers to discuss social justice issues specific to Black culture. I also continued to host the

Capital City Youth Football Coaches Clinic. I'll never forget the weekend before we were scheduled to return to school from spring break 2020. We had our fifth annual clinic and banquet at Hudl in downtown Lincoln, and then the next day, everything shut down. We did not return to school.

The world was in lockdown. We were confined to our homes, not knowing how long it would last. The level of fear continued to gain intensity as days, weeks, and then months passed. As a campus supervisor, I'm not supervising any kids, right? I'm thinking, what am I going to do with my time?

I decided to use the time for research and some basic reading. I focused on Africa and made it my goal to relearn African history. I did not feel that I had been taught African history thoroughly. I felt a sense of responsibility to educate myself because I was in charge of the African American Caucus and felt like I was at a deficit when it came to talking about the history of Africa, and I wanted to be better.

I also was a part of an organization called I Ask, I Act. We were just getting things off the ground when Minneapolis cops killed George Floyd on May 25, 2020. I was sitting at home with the rest of the world as we watched a Black man's murder be televised. It was on every news outlet—there wasn't an escape from the footage. Then my phone began to blow up. I got text messages and nonstop phone calls from people asking me what they could do. Everyone felt like they should be doing something. The calls were from a diverse group of people, and it seemed they were ready to be proactive.

I provided the best advice or ideas I could at the time. Still, it really made me begin to think not just about what people could do in these situations but about what we, as African Americans, can do because we are the group largely affected by these social injustices. We were constantly bombarded with images like rapid fire. George Floyd just happened to be the peak of things, but the years leading up to this incident involved a list of names and videos of injustices we saw consistently against our community. It seemed like these acts were becoming an epidemic.

George Floyd sparked a fire in me. I suddenly had the motivation to do the stuff I had been putting off for such a long time. I picked up a book called *The Rebirth of African Civilization* by Chancellor Williams, and from that moment on, I doubled down on my studies and did a deep dive into our history. I wanted to learn more about Africa. Not only learn, but I also wanted to visit the country and immerse myself in its culture.

I had stacks of books about Africa and read them all. The books led to meaningful conversations rooted in truth, and from there, I continued to expand my knowledge. *The autobiography of Malcolm X* became my favorite book. I've read it several times. I came across authors like John Henrik Clarke, James Baldwin, and Walter Rodney, and before I knew it, I went down a rabbit hole. It was not my intention to get so immersed in literature, but I am glad I did because it made me rethink my understanding of African history. I had to go back and relearn African history and, with that, also learn the elements of systemic racism. I wanted to be equipped to answer when someone asked me a question about race, or someone said an act was racist. I needed to understand and identify the actual mechanisms and triggers that are used to implement systemic racism.

The study and research became an obsession, so much so that it started to feel stressful. In the middle of all this, I had to learn a valuable lesson: I needed to take care of myself physically and mentally. I had to establish healthy self-care practices. I didn't realize the amount of stress I was putting on myself with all the research and the mental and emotional toll of the George Floyd incident, as well as being on lockdown. I shifted my focus to include learning and understanding the importance of exercise, meditation, nutrition, breathing, and community service. There was a shift in my mindset, and within this shift, I created what I call the four pillars of understanding. These pillars became the baseline of a new lifestyle that was emerging for me.

MY FOUR PILLARS of Understanding

1. Relearn African history.

2. Understand the mechanics of systemic racism.

3. Practice self-care.

4. Stay involved in the community.

IT HAS BEEN my experience that as long as a person does those four things, not necessarily in that order but continually, they will be better equipped to deal with microaggressions and help those around them when faced with the stress of social injustices on the local level as well as on larger scales. George Floyd unleashed something. Times were changing, and people came together around the nation. Social injustices were being challenged around the world as people became fed up. People were using their platforms to speak out against these issues and no longer choosing to stand still. Instead, they took to the streets to protest and let their voices be heard. The images of protests were everywhere, and it was inspiring to see that people were ready to have uncomfortable conversations but also put action behind their words.

Another big push for me was that I had become exhausted from being neutral to everything that was going on around me. I generally stayed away from politically charged issues, but at some point, I decided it was time for me to get out of my comfort zone because being neutral was more of me shutting things out, and it wasn't healthy.

I was making every excuse not to continue my education. I told myself that I was too old to go back. I had earned my associate's degree from the local community college in 2011. It had been such a struggle (especially the math) that I talked myself into believing it was good enough. But I strongly believe that if you know better, you do better, and it was time for me to do better. George Floyd's murder gave me the final push I needed to get shit done. I am unsure if I would've ever gotten the motivation to go back to school or begin the research and study had we not been confined to our homes. Having enough time wasn't an issue because all I had for weeks was time to get things done. I am sure many people developed new hobbies and skills during the shutdown, and we all had to learn to take care of ourselves. We also learned to value the things we may have taken for granted, especially connection with other people.

My thoughts and efforts are always with the African American community and how I can help. I would be remiss, however, to believe that I should just focus my energy on our community alone because, speaking honestly, if I make that my primary focus, I'll be disappointed every time. By focusing on the broader community, we get what is known as the curb-cut effect. The curb-cut effect started in San Francisco. When the city made curb cuts at intersections to allow wheelchair access, they discovered the cuts had reciprocal impacts. The elderly community and delivery drivers could also benefit from the curb cuts. The curb cut is the way I look at my community. I have my community on my mind while focusing on a broader spectrum, which then reaches more people.

For example, with the mental health initiatives and education programs I'm working on as part of Civic Nebraska, our community was on my mind when the programs were created and continues to be on my mind. I hope these programs attract the attention of the African American community, but they are meant to serve everyone. The goal is to create change on a larger scale.

I must admit, if someone had told the little brown, adopted, abused, angry, academically mediocre boy raised in Omaha that he would become a man with a voice for change, a love for people, and a passion for advocating for our community, I would've laughed. Yet here I stand, and I wouldn't change anything about my journey.

IDENTITY

GHANA, WEST AFRICA

TOP & MIDDLE: With Students at Badu Bonsoe School
BOTTOM LEFT: At Crocodile Lagoon
BOTTOM RIGHT: Meeting with prince

CHAPTER 24
AN ESSAY FROM THE JOURNALIST

WITH OLUSEYE

I STRONGLY BELIEVE that everyone who has ever known Kwame Gyamfi should re-meet him again in their lifetime—his parents, his family, his fellow inmates, and co-workers—all those who knew him when he lived his life as Shannon White. I can't tell if he feels some cringe when someone calls him that. I didn't ask. However, if there is one thing I know about names, I know that old names feel grating in the ears of those who previously bore them. And a new name, when called, sounds rhythmic to the ears of the bearer.

I also know that Shannon White never belonged to the man whose soul longed for a name that fit, a name that said who he was. On more than one occasion, Shannon White was assumed to be a Caucasian woman.

Kwame, the name he now bears, seems somewhat like a prophecy pronounced with some sort of spiritual inclinations. Listening to the story of the birth of this new name, you will agree it wasn't a mere coincidence.

My first meetings with Kwame were via Zoom. From the way he spoke from his heart, you can tell that as Shannon, he lived an adventurous life. A life of gangs in North Omaha, being sent to a juvenile detention center, and failing out of programs meant to rehabilitate. Or, too, his time at Boys Town. Shannon did live a life—a life that Kwame now rewrites by telling his story and helping others pull through.

The day I physically met Kwame was a Wednesday as the writers working on this book gathered to meet the man whose life we had explored over hours on Zoom. At 7:01 p.m., Kwame gaily walked into the living room, giving everyone the warmest embrace you could imagine. He smelled good and wore a white long-sleeved shirt and carbon-like pants. On his head sat a fedora hat. He moved around the room, totally at home. Or, I should say, he made us feel like a family. I perused him keenly before he finally settled on a chair at the corner, right beside our hostess. Before this event, Zoom was my only contact with Kwame, and I honestly didn't know what to expect. It didn't take long for me to realize that for Kwame, everyone is family, irrespective of where and how he met them. During this meeting, my mind paced like a recorder, rewinding all the things Kwame had told me in our many Zoom conversations.

His aura in the room commanded some form of authority as we charged him with questions for clarity. I, along with other writers, have a slice of Kwame that we want the world to see. And for the world to see this, we must see Kwame first for the man he was and now for the man he is. Believe me, there were no traces of the man he was. Well, none I noticed except for some pictures spread on the dining table that acted as filler to the epoch of his life.

As conversation glided, Kwame began retelling these stories of himself like a recounter, taking me back to his history. Of course, I knew of his anger, theft, and arrest, but more was to be revealed

—most especially more to be discovered at the point where he himself encountered a newness.

Without sentiment, I do believe his life is a journey, perhaps preordained. I also believe that I may not have met Kwame as the man that he is now—a man who inspires, a man who has a story to tell—if I had not first met Shannon White. The man I met is living the remaining part of his life with a new name and a distinguished purpose.

Kwame Gyamfi is a rare name among the African Americans that I know. I am from Nigeria and have met those with the names Asante, Kofi, and all, but none with a peculiar story like Kwame's about how they got their names. I say peculiar because many African Americans I've met are curious about their ancestry, tracing their roots back to Africa. This same curiosity began Kwame's quest, but his initial purpose was to learn more about Africa to tell better stories of the continent and to understand his own history. After the hurdles in his life, especially his incarceration, he began a reconciliation of helping kids on sports teams and in high schools, kids who find themselves in the same labyrinth he was caught in. He knew that to talk about Africa properly, to reconcile his African roots, and help many whom he is canvassing for, to make them see the importance and the dignifying attributes of their color, the journey doesn't end with Ancestry.com, but a visit to Africa. For Kwame, this visit was to West Africa—to Ghana, where he traced his origin.

I listened as Kwame spoke about his dissatisfaction with how African history was taught, even more as he oversaw the African American Caucus and led discussions about the continent. He felt he needed to have a proper fill of things that are devoid in textbooks. His venture was relearning, unlearning, and experiencing Africa for himself. I do believe that only a lived experience can relate with another lived experience, so the universe was orchestrating his destiny.

I believe in providence for this journey because the trip became feasible when Kwame received a settlement after his car got T-boned while he was driving home from school. The convergence of COVID and his role at Lincoln High becoming unsettled plunged him into research, and he began to make plans for this trip. The first place he checked was a Facebook group of traveling enthusiasts going on similar African quests to Ghana. Fate led him to discover Bright, a twenty-six-year-old, who would later become his tour guide in Ghana.

My heart raced when Kwame mentioned how he met Bright and paid upfront to have his undivided attention for the twenty-one days in Ghana. My heart skipped because I've seen too much. I know of the long-held prejudices that African Americans have for their fellow Black men, most especially those who are from Africa, and vice versa. The brown paper bag test is just one example of Blacks discriminating against one another based on the shade of one's skin. This colorism separates us into groups that are lighter or darker than a grocery sack. I was surprised to learn that Kwame took the risk of seeing someone of his race without the prejudice that Blacks in Africa are generally known for. For Kwame, who was tracing his roots and seeking answers, trust must come into play to find those. Perhaps meeting Bright is another important clue to show that the universe grants the quest of any seeker by connecting them with the right humans on their journey.

As Kwame spoke about his journey to Accra, Ghana, he mentioned the turbulence. His way would not be smooth. The trip to Ghana began in Chicago; then he flew to Brussels in Belgium, where he had a twenty-four-hour layover. Personally, layovers during travel are times for reflection and the questioning that can arise while one is engaging in a trip. Perhaps Kwame thought of this, too, once he landed after the eight-hour bumpy ride. He didn't say. He did say he took this time to explore Brussels.

From Brussels, Kwame took a seven-hour flight to Accra. I paused at the point when he arrived in Ghana and received a message that Bright had to attend to a family emergency. A part of me honestly feared that Kwame was being too trusting, but this is due to my prejudices about people of my race. Kwame opened my eyes to something I had never really thought about myself: the prestige of one's heritage. Westerners, Kwame noted, are proud to tell anyone who cares to listen about their ancestry. They will tell you that their grandparents or great-grandparents came from Ireland, or Germany, or wherever. But for the African American, the association of their ancestry to the continent is ineffable. While this seemed like an African American issue, I honestly feel it is a universal issue plaguing every person of color.

My stereotype soon became unlived when Bright's uncle showed up and attended to Kwame the way any human would have. He was charitable and hospitable, taking him everywhere he needed to go. And as they say in Africa, "they made him feel at home."

Navigating the situation in an unfamiliar country wasn't the beginning of survival for Kwame. At fourteen, he had run away from home to live in an abandoned house where he had to tap electricity from a neighbor and improvise ways of toileting and finding food. In the continent, most especially in some West African countries, electricity and water are not always available. Perhaps his time in the abandoned house was preparation for the future. As the English would say, a harbinger. I am sure many in Ghana wondered if Kwame was from the States because of how easily he blended in. Take for instance, not only navigating the power supply but also having to bathe by scooping water from a container. They must have wondered what manner of man he was to have enjoyed these situations.

Another thing that struck me during this conversation with Kwame was when he said he didn't see himself as Black in Ghana because everyone looked like him. There is an honest vulnerability here and a lesson, if one will. Back in Omaha, Nebraska, North America, Kwame is defined by many things, and first for being Black. The color identity hangs over him like a cloud of remembrance that makes one see it before they start seeing him as a person. However, in Ghana, that wasn't so. The people frolicked around him to learn from him rather than stare at him. He came seeking stories, but the journey of the twenty-one days revealed a lifelong truth he will forever be telling, which will influence his policies and strengthen his advocacy.

To get to see Otumfuo Badu Bonsu XV, the titular ruler of Ahanta land, as he had planned, Kwame needed to see some things beforehand. One was to tour the king's school as a way of integrating himself not just into the culture but also into the environment. Kwame's aim for this trip was to be a better recounter of African American history, and if he must be a better recounter back in the US, he needed to give these twenty-one days his rapt attention. Before leaving for Ghana, one of his greatest challenges was to ensure that African American students were seen for the essence of their being beyond being Black. And, of course, his story of abandonment, abuse, school truancy, Horace Mann Park, gangs, theft, and prison not only shaped him but reformed his mind to help others, mostly Black students. While Kwame sees that all students matter, the ravaging issue of the school-to-prison pipeline is most common among students of color. His examples were vivid, not just from his story but also those from some of the students who make bad decisions because of dysfunctional homes, the society they grew up in, or just a lackadaisical approach toward life.

I wasn't surprised when he began describing his experiences at the king's school in Ghana. He was blown away by the rapt attention the students paid to their teachers, the coordination, and the serenity of the environment. All the students stood to greet him and raised their hands in unison to answer the teacher's questions. These were new school experiences, and Kwame was enthused by everything he saw. The bewilderment of all these was that this school had more than 2,000 students! Could he bring back anything he could incorporate at Lincoln High?

Another sight he won't forget was the boy who was cutting the grass outside the school.

"Why is he out here?" Kwame asked.

"Oh, he was having problems today. He didn't want to do school," a teacher replied.

If there is one thing I genuinely love about Kwame's sequence of events, apart from his vulnerability to each of his life's happenings, Kwame doesn't shy away from hiding his feelings and surprises. He expressed outrage at the surcharges he experienced in his daily transactions with people who looked like him and the inappropriateness when the headmaster wanted a tip. I also believe this is telling all parts of the realities because Kwame's road to rediscovering Africa was never an easy route, especially because of the risk and naivety he faced throughout his journey.

In retrospect, when Kwame began telling his story about the desire to travel to Africa and learn the stories from a first-hand point of view, I thought that was all it was, but as he further revealed the events, I saw layer upon layer of purpose. Sometimes, all one must do is just leap, and that's what Kwame did.

"SO HOW DID your name become Kwame?" I asked.

Kwame's face beamed at this point, delighted to tell the story of his rebirth. While the experience at the king's school was for him to learn about a culture of disciplinarian modification, the experience at the palace was for him to receive a purpose for the mandate.

I am an African, and I know the importance of a name. Every child is given a name according to happenings around the parents or a foretelling of the child's birth. In other words, every named child has a purpose.

Kwame arrived at the palace of the Ahanta at noon. The wall artifacts caught his attention—pictures depicting the history of the king, his forefathers, and his council of chiefs. Twice, Kwame said that he felt at ease in the palace—a feeling of being at home. But inside him, he described a thirst, a brokenness, at not having a language for home, his roots.

When the chiefs welcomed him, he didn't hide his ecstasy, saying, "Bright went down on his knees to pay a form of reverence." Kwame followed suit, and when he was asked to introduce himself, I was stunned when he said he began with an apology for not being able to speak in the dialect.

Now, every African child has a dialect. A dialect is a native language of a tribe, and a member of a tribe is expected to learn the language. Since Kwame was able to identify his roots in Ahanta land, it was expected that as a "son of the soil," he should be able to communicate in the native language. During the transatlantic trade, captured Africans who worked on plantations took their languages with them. Still, over time, the use of these African Indigenous languages in North America declined, discarded tools that lost their place in the New World.

It was proper for Kwame to apologize, and he wasn't being dramatic. It is a symbol of a returned son who had long sojourned but found his way back home.

"Their next reaction shocked me," Kwame said.

"They formed a cluster amongst themselves and, after some minutes of deliberation proclaimed me 'Kwame Gyamfi.'" The name means great warrior born on a Saturday.

Kwame smiled. He had indeed been born on a Saturday.

Coincidental or divine? I observed that Kwame didn't want to tag this pronouncement as a divine orchestration, and I understand. Yet I believe that some things don't have to be named because they are inexplicable.

This naming began a change for Shannon, now Kwame. Then, the eldest chief made another pronouncement.

"Kwame, your life will change after this visit," he said as Bright translated.

During the meeting with these chiefs, no English was spoken. All Kwame heard was a translation from Bright. While I think Bright did a good job endeavoring to translate all the chiefs' words, or prophesy, as I can choose to call it, I also wonder if some of the words weren't lost in translation.

I wonder if more was said and less was translated. I sense this because most African sentences are wrapped in proverbs, and these proverbs are witty words that carry either an additional or an intensified meaning. To say Kwame knew all that was given to him during his meeting with these chiefs is to miss some nuances and meanings that English sentences cannot comprehend.

After seeing these chiefs, Kwame waited for the next two hours for Otumfuo Badu Bonsu XV, the traditional ruler of the Ahanta. I wondered if Kwame's patience was tested. I am not sure anyone has to wait that long to see any figure in the US. But he waited, he had to experience the process of meeting an African monarch whom he will now forever refer to as, "My King."

"What was going through your mind?" I asked.

"I was blown away, and looking around, hurriedly taking pictures because I also do not want them to think I was only interested in that," he said, chuckling.

And as if he was anticipating revealing the moment he finally met the king, he gently cut in with "anyway" just when my vocal cords were forming the next question.

"Anyway," he said, "Bright then informed me that the king now was ready to see me."

The elegant chamber of the king is forever a place Kwame will remember. He and the king spoke at great length in English, discussing Black situations both in Africa and in the diaspora.

The other core of the meeting was a discussion of education and its implementation. For Kwame, this wasn't all about meeting an African monarch. This was an intellectual discussion on how he could take an African pedagogical tool, which had already mesmerized him, back to the United States.

However, just before he left the king's chamber, Osei Tutu II looked at Kwame and said, "Your life will never remain the same after this."

Kwame paused, reenacting the scene and the way the sentence came to him.

"How did you feel hearing this for the second time?" I asked.

"Honestly, I was startled because he said the same thing that the oldest chief said even without being in the meeting."

I pondered the discussion and experience with the king as Kwame told me of his last days in Accra and with the Ahanta tribe. He mentioned documenting these events in a journal, a journal I earnestly wish to see. He spoke about the tears he shed. Healing tears, Bright called them.

The journey to Accra was a rebirth. Even Kwame agrees. Some may view the happenings as coincidental or normal, and that's fine. But with a critical look, one would agree that things like the name, the seeming prophesy by the oldest chief, and the confirmation from the king weren't just things that happened by chance.

After the twenty-one-day trip, Kwame's return to the United States began with a newness within him, one he couldn't describe but could be felt. It was a beginning, a chance to start living in the reality of his new name. Others accepting that reality could be daunting.

His loving wife was the first to openly embrace her husband's new name. She instantly adapted to calling him Kwame Gyamfi.

"Oh, your adopted parents, how did they react?" I asked.

"My father never really liked the name. He made a joke about it."

"And others?" I asked.

"Others are coming along. Some still call me by my old name, those who knew me from the hood. My best friend also didn't call me Kwame for a long time."

Kwame's mission to Africa, however, was not to have a name change but to better carry the task ahead for him.

You see, most people who lead a campaign of some sort had to shed a part of themselves that people were used to. Perhaps this was the essence of the name change. A name that will carry the identity of someone worthy to tell his story and help students who are like him not to make the same mistakes that he made and for them to see the beautiful sides of life that can be achieved with due diligence and having the right mentors.

I also see the twenty-one days of Kwame as a journey to his transformation. It may look like a fairytale, but knowing the essence and the importance of mysticism and spirituality in Africa, these are what have equipped the Kwame that I first saw on a Zoom call, then later in flesh, clad in his white apparel.

The journey of Kwame doesn't end with his visit to Africa. He is a traveler, a sojourner like every one of us, one whose experience had molded him into the man we see today. He has worn every aspect of his life like an emblem, inseparable parts of him. From abandonment by his birth parents, to an orphanage, then an adoptive family marred by abuse, to North Omaha, gang influence, Boys Town, Bellingham, Job Corps, theft, imprisonment— all make a worthy story about a Black boy's road to freedom, healing, and helping others who might be caught in the same labyrinth.

I thought our conversation was almost over, but Kwame jerked forward like he remembered a part of his story also worthy of telling. As a writer and a freelance journalist, one of the things I fear after every interview is a question that puzzles me until the final publication of a story. Honestly, I am glad Kwame revealed this part, an important prelude to the meat of his entire existence.

The journey from Shannon to Kwame is also his story in Bellingham, Washington. The way he described Bellingham seemed a foreshadowing of his trip to Accra, Ghana. In Bellingham, he explored some deep parts of himself: his will for sports, his quest for life's vitality and vigor, and, again, youthful adventure. But it was a place he learned some lifelong lessons. All this while, he has been a seeker, even as an angry child when societal influence and family circumstances made him an explosive time bomb who made some hasty decisions that cost him a lot.

At some points, Kwame referred to himself as a "wannabe." He threw this word around several times, but it was not until I began juxtaposing his trip to Accra, Ghana, with all the experiences he had shared that I began to connect the pieces like a puzzle.

It is amazing how, as humans, we sometimes use descriptions that unknowingly foretell our future. And when Kwame used "wannabe," I believe that was what his soul had been yearning for —he wanted an identity, a purpose, even amongst the deafening voices of discrimination, violence, and the societal breakdowns affecting him growing up as an African American child.

Boys Town was supposed to rehab him, reform him into a good man, devoid of his teenage rage and violence. His background had been tough, similar to his experience and choices. His houseparents were fired after taking him on a football recruiting trip to Buena Vista University in Storm Lake, Iowa. So, after he graduated, he followed them to Bellingham, where they invited him into their home and gave him an idea of what a good family could look like. But his rehabilitation is a process, a newness that began from the rear. Kwame may not have noticed the interrelatedness of these life scenarios: Truancy and eventually dropping out of Burke High School, failing at group homes, and never finding an ideal mentor until Mr. Crawford at Boys Town. This alone is a testament to the advocacy that Kwame now gives high school boys and other teenagers he meets. I listened as he also told the story of Lincoln High and how he tries to mediate and instill discipline in the kids, most especially the Black kids.

"I feel like I am called for this," he said when he also talked about the school-to-prison pipeline and the introduction of the police force in the school system. While he says he understands the importance of this to mitigate violence, he strongly believes some of the issues could easily be curbed with proper mentorship.

I looked at Kwame again as he stood and ushered us to the rectangular-shaped dining room. He moved around the room, opening the folder on the table and sorting the pictures to match the years.

Compared to the man I see, these pictures reveal two different people. I also won't doubt that his new name had had a huge impact on him, and this time, in a positive way. You see, during earlier interviews, while listening to the projection of his life as he had described the anger and resentment, the feeling he finally described as "a wannabe" permeates the entire theme of his story. As I looked at the pictures he chose and reflected on the stories he shared with us, I saw that they all led from "wannabe" to the new identity he now bears.

Kwame's journey has admittedly not been an easy route. He could have angrily changed his name by himself. Merely recalling that he had to pay rent to his father to live in an inadequate basement after returning to North Omaha might be a good reason for a child to disassociate from a family. Also, returning after his incarceration could have been the straw that broke the camel's back, yet none of this happened. It is agreed that he was angry at himself and with his adoptive father, who had also been his greatest critic, but never had he thought during this period to detach himself from him.

Perhaps what Kwame had been seeking through all these years was also seeking him. While we may contest the process of his purpose seeking after him, and some may argue the fact of how bad choices finally straighten out a teenage boy, yet if it would rest on the beam of predestination, his stories re-echoed that Wednesday night, to me sounded like a predestination.

Of course, those experiences were not interesting. Having to watch his parents' rage at him and seeing football—the only thing that gave him a sense of purpose at the time—ripped away due to injury? Incarceration?

But like the name Gyamfi, which means warrior, maybe he had been called to fight a system all his life. And for him to know and properly fight this system that tends to clip the wings of Black American children, he needed to be caught in the loop of the system. He needed to feel the brunt of the system and never be swept off by the fury at Horace Mann Park. How better would he be able to tell a story of freedom to the kids he now mentors?

"Talking about Africa made me to want to travel to Africa," he said.

And yes, unbeknownst to him, the thing he was seeking had always been seeking him to bequeath on him a name.

TWO-FACED

JAN BRETZ

Simon says, "Move on back

you Black" I remember

I'm just four, riding a bus to

an orphanage

called The Farm.

No bearings. No brother.

One day my face

graces a poster.

I'm on TV. Just like that,

I'm adopted by a White woman

and a man with a face like mine,

reunited with my brother.

At fifty I read the adoption records

of a closed adoption.

Names blacked out. Redacted.

Am I blacked out or

Just Black?

It's years 'til I'd learn

to forgive the unnamed mother,

the one who gave me birth,

hold both anger and

perspective in my hands.

The bottle and the needle fed her.

She threw sacks of snacks

on the floor when

she'd walk out the door.

No water.

My small face faced a

porcelain pool meant for excrement.

I slurped. Face in a toilet.

became my place, my habit,

years after when I'd freakout.

This water refused

to quench my thirst.

How long would my face

mean shit, my name mean

nothing?

How long 'til I'd raise my chin,

marry, hold babies and jobs,

fly to Africa

sit at the bedside of a king,

be named by a people who claim me?

How long 'til I'd wear a face

of grace for those I love,

family, friends, strangers?

Who'd imagine, who'd surmise

I'd be remade? Reborn

Kwame, "born on a Saturday"

become Kwame the Overcomer

MY ADOPTIVE MOM

TOP: With my daughter at my wedding.

LEFT: With my adoptive father.

EPILOGUE

THE FUNERAL HOME was nearly empty. Just me, my wife, and our children. My mother, the woman who had been my anchor, was gone. At ninety-two, she had lived a long life, but her last months had been spent bedridden and in hospice. I hadn't known. My father never called to tell me. I never got to say goodbye.

Instead, I received a single phone call after her passing—a cold announcement of her death.

Standing in that room, I expected grief, but what filled the space instead was something darker—the weight of a lifetime of manipulation, control, and emotional distance. My father stood before us, and as I braced myself for words of remembrance, for a prayer for my mother, he did what he always did; he made it about himself. He prayed not for her but for me, for his son to learn obedience. My wife and children looked at me, their eyes filled with the same disbelief I felt. I tuned him out, but the damage had already settled in my bones. After the burial, I sat in the car and screamed. The silence that followed told me everything. My family understood now. They had seen it firsthand.

Later, my wife told me about the conversation she had with him. She had gone to see him, maybe hoping for something I had long given up on. In that conversation, he admitted to what I had always known but never heard from his own lips. He had been jealous of my relationship with my mother. He had seen me as a rival rather than a son. Anywhere she went, I followed, and that attention, in his eyes, had been stolen from him.

For a moment, I thought there was an opening, a crack in the armor he had built around himself. My wife arranged for us to meet, to talk, but when the time came, he had already rewritten history. He had prayed on it and told her that reconciliation wasn't necessary. He didn't think he had anything to apologize for. He offered lunch, not as a bridge, but as a final power play, a way to make sure I understood that he would never take responsibility.

He had rewritten history in other ways, too—every disagreement, every time I asserted myself. He rewrote the will. Less for me. Less for my children. Eventually, we were erased entirely. My younger brother, too. My father's form of punishment, his last act of control.

There were other accusations, absurd ones. That I had taken over a house, that I had trashed a property. That I had kept his grandchildren from him. Lies layered on top of lies, twisted to fit his narrative.

But the truth was clear. My father was never going to change. He had spent decades alienating people, pushing them away until, in the end, no one remained but the son he had spent a lifetime trying to break. And even then, I was only there because I had no choice but to be the one to lay my mother to rest.

Walking away from that funeral home, I knew with certainty that I would not follow in his footsteps. The cycle ended with me.

TOP: Receiving bachelor's degree from Doane College, May 2025 **BOTTOM:** Speaking at various civic and educational events.

ABOUT KWAME

Kwame Gyamfi has served in many roles during his eighteen years in public education. Working with public and private schools since 2007, he has been a campus supervisor, high school football coach, African American caucus sponsor, equity, inclusion and diversity facilitator, and student advocate. For nearly two decades, he has coached football at the youth through college levels. He helped write the African studies curriculum for Lincoln High School in 2021.

In his current role on the Malone Center Leadership Team, Kwame is the School Community Coordinator, serving as the after-school principal running the Community Learning Center at Lincoln Northeast High School. He also reviews legislation and its potential impact on the community. Kwame creates quality programming with a focus on civic engagement through the use of STEAM, mentorship, and social-emotional learning programming for a diverse group of students. He is the creator of the Human Connection Strategies program at Civic Nebraska and the student-driven Future Harvest program at Northeast High School.

Kwame is currently the Co-Chair of the Lincoln Memorial Day Committee and a recent Citizens University Fellow. He is also an award-winning writer, an African historian, a public speaker, an artist, and a business owner.

THE WRITERS

FROM TOP: Kwame Gyamfi, LaShawnda Nimox, S.C. Huddleston, Jan Bretz, Oluseye Fakinlede, and Cindy Conger

ABOUT THE WRITERS

Jan Bretz has always loved story. It may be what led her to pursue a secondary teaching license at Indiana State with a concentration in English and what was then called Speech and Drama. Jan taught high school speech, English, and theatre in Lincoln, Nebraska, and was an assistant speech coach at a local school. She's been a volunteer coach for TEDxLincoln and TEDx-Omaha, and provided presentation workshops for businesses and organizations, including The Nebraska Storytelling Festival. She has also coached individuals, led a writing class, and taught speech class at the Nebraska Correctional Center for Women.

Oluseye Fakinlede is a journalist and writer from Nigeria, who is deeply passionate about storytelling and human-interest reporting. His work thoughtfully explores compelling themes around sexual identities and religion, which form the heart of both his literary and journalistic pursuits. He currently writes and resides in Lincoln, Nebraska.

S.C. Huddleston lives in Nebraska with his ravishing wife and two ravenous pups. Coming from a humble and unprivileged background, he resolved to change his stars when he was of age to try. He received a Bachelor of Science in Political Science and Public Law at the University of Nebraska. He went on to earn a Master of Fine Arts in Creative Writing at Southern New Hampshire University. Huddleston is an avid reader and writer of contemporary fiction. He was shortlisted in the 2021 Vocal+ Fiction Awards Challenge for his short story "September." His short story, "Don't Be Afraid," was published in *The Penmen Review*. He has also written novels in literary fiction, historical fiction, and YA fantasy. Huddleston is an editor and proofreader for numerous award-winning authors and professors. Huddleston also tutors high school students in English, literature, and writing.

LaShawnda Nimox, known as Shawn by family and friends, was born and raised in the cities of Chicago and Maywood, Illinois. She is a single parent of three children and currently resides in Lincoln, Nebraska. She works as an education advocate for African American youth and families. She is an established author of her own poetry book, *No Filter,* and leads a youth book club and STEM Club at the only Black cultural center in Lincoln. LaShawnda has made it her life's work to be an advocate of literacy and representation for her community and beyond.

Cindy Conger has spent the last two decades helping writers bring their books to print. Her background in journalism and love of story compels her to help others shape their manuscripts. She comes alongside best-selling authors and those with one-off memoirs or passion projects to help share stories across the human spectrum. When she's not editing or helping writers query agents, she is most likely watching sports. She resides in Lincoln, Nebraska.

NOTES

CHAPTER 9

i. Bahnsen, Kylie. "Forgotten History: Is It Time for a Name Change?", Burke Bee, November 26, 2019. Accessed online, January 25, 2025. https://bhspress.com/1454/opinion/forgotten-history-is-it-time-for-a-name-change/

ii. "As momentum gains to rename Omaha high school, historian examines Harry Burke's racial past," KMTV News, posted June 26, 2020. Accessed online, January 25, 2025, https://www.3newsnow.com/news/local-news/as-momentum-gains-to-rename-omaha-high-school-historian-examines-harry-burkes-racial-past

www.ingramcontent.com/pod-product-compliance
Lightning Source LLC
Chambersburg PA
CBHW071732120626
46550CB00002B/489